In an age where value is often determined by the number of Twitter followers and Facebook "likes" a person has, the idea of embracing obscurity seems about as outdated as an old rotary dial phone. Not to mention, social networking has made it possible to broadcast the details of our day down to what we had for breakfast and the playlist of songs we listened to on our lunch break. It's all beginning to be a bit too much. I applaud whoever wrote this book for reminding us all of our ultimate purpose: To make much of God and less of ourselves. This book is an absolute treasure that should be on every Christian's nightstand. Permanently.

—Vicki Courtney, a fellow author, who would have rather gone unnamed to embrace obscurity

We live in a celebrity-obsessed culture. And let's be real, the church isn't all that different. In fact, in the church we often make the case that influence is something to be pursued; the greater our influence, the greater our impact for Christ. Yet, what does it mean to make much of ourselves in order to make much of Him, instead of trusting Him to make much of Himself—despite us. *Embracing Obscurity* is incredibly powerful as it reminds us to question whether we are building our own self-importance or finding it in Christ. Are we willing to be obscure so that Christ is exalted? How can we say no?

—Jen Hatmaker, author of *7: An Experimental Mutiny Against Excess*

Our lives can exalt only one person. This book challenged me to consider who, for me, that one person was. Am I willing to embrace obscurity for Jesus? If only one person can receive attention in my life, is it Him? This book helped me marvel again at the Christ who embraced obscurity for us. His

humiliation led to our exaltation. When we understand that, how can we not say, "He must increase, but I must decrease!"

—JD Greear, Lead Pastor, the Summit Church
Twitter: @jdgreear @summitrdu

It is a paradoxical sign of the times that a book advocating the virtues of anonymity yet requires named endorsements in order to be properly marketable. Thus, it is with some sense of irony, if not incoherence, that I commend this work. We live in an age where self-promotion is the norm and where even many sincere Christians have bought into this culture with enthusiasm. Yet the message of this important book is that such self-promotion is not simply a neutral cultural tool but is in fact antithetical to biblical Christianity. This is a timely call to modesty, privacy, and humility. It is painful but necessary reading that is likely to be hated, disparaged, or simply ignored by the very people who most need to heed its message.

—Carl R. Trueman, Westminster Theological Seminary

If American evangelicalism is like a football team, with different positions and players, *Embracing Obscurity* is the 300-pound linebacker lurking over the middle. It hits hard. There were sentences in this book that stopped me cold. Conclusions from its provocative critique will vary, but the book is prophetic and needed. I'm not anonymous in recommending this text, but I'm definitely stirred to embrace the gospel that knocks us down like Saul, frees us from sin and death, and turns vainglorious somebodies into glorious nobodies.

—Owen Strachan, Assistant Professor of
Christian Theology and Church History;
coauthor, *Essential Edwards Collection*

Many of us are drunk right now, intoxicated with a desire to be respected, honored, and widely known. And yet this intoxication derails our ability to give God the respect, honor, and renown that He so rightly deserves. For this reason, the author of *Embracing Obscurity* argues that we must renounce this desire to build our own kingdom and, in so doing, we will find unspeakable joy and freedom in Christ. If you are fighting the temptation to build your own kingdom—like I am—you need to buy this book and take its thesis to heart.

—Bruce Riley Ashford, Dean of The College Research Fellow, Southeastern Baptist Theological Seminary

Embracing Obscurity is a tremendous challenge to the greatest hindrance to fulfilling the Great Commission, namely PLEASURE. I must get this book into the hands of all the people I lead.

—Johnny Hunt, pastor, First Baptist Church, Woodstock, Georgia

Embracing Obscurity challenges us to cultivate a joyful sense of contentment in the truth that the One who matters most already knows you. Being known by Him is enough.

—Trevin Wax, managing editor of The Gospel Project, author of *Counterfeit Gospels* and *Holy Subversion*

Embracing Obscurity may change the way you view the authentic Christian life. It pierced my heart with the simple truth that I do not suffer from a lack of self-confidence but from an abundance of self-importance. Can I be content with relative obscurity so that Christ may be made more famous?! A haunting question to be sure. A worthwhile question no doubt. So, be prepared to be made uncomfortable in a good way.

—Daniel L. Akin, president of Southeastern Baptist Theological Seminary

Pride is the plague of the human heart, and like most people, I long to be known. I long to enter into the kingdom of heaven riding the white horse, crown on my head, sword in my hand. I want to be the self-sufficient Christian. The gospel call, though, is a call to enter the kingdom on my knees. It is because of this that I am deeply grateful for the unknown author who not only embraced obscurity, but who lovingly calls us to do the same in this book. Please reed, weep, and walk this way.

—Micah Fries, pastor, Frederick Boulevard

A man who won't put his name on his book greatly authenticates his thesis "All for His glory, none of mine." Only the cross has the wondrous attraction. Not me, not my church, not my glory. America's Christians and their leaders need no message more than this, "He must increase; I must decrease. Completely."

—John Bisagno, pastor emeritus of First Baptist Church, Houston, Texas and author of *Pastor's Handbook*

EMBRACING OBSCURITY

BECOMING NOTHING IN LIGHT OF GOD'S EVERYTHING

ANONYMOUS

B&H

PUBLISHING GROUP

NASHVILLE, TENNESSEE

To my Humble King,
who has ever taught by example.

And to all those who, like me,
have clamored long enough.

Contents

INTRODUCTION

Why Embracing Obscurity?

What do you, me, a student, a musician, a stay-at-home mom, a laid-off blue-collar worker, a pastor, and a successful entrepreneur all have in common?

We're drunk.

In our defense the epidemic is so common that most of us don't even know we're under the influence. We're confused, blinded, and wandering around like sailors at dawn; but, then again, so is everyone else, so why should we be alarmed? But this unsuspected poison is simultaneously numbing us, diverting our attention from the kingdom and undermining the gospel of Christ.

We're drunk all right. We're intoxicated with a desire to be known, recognized, appreciated, and respected. We crave to be a "somebody" and do notable things, to achieve our dreams and gain the admiration of others. To be something—*anything*—other than nothing.

Whether you're an athlete, postal worker, missionary, or government employee, haven't you felt the insatiable draw of notoriety? Where do you think that comes from? We live in a culture that bases significance on how celebrated, or common, we are. And now the church seems to have followed suit. This is serious stuff. It's serious because of its source. It's just the sort of lie that Satan—the father of lies—manufactures and sells best. It's not too shocking. It can be justified and religious-sized and explained away easily enough. But it kills with the same force as the "big sins" from which we distance ourselves.

We all feel it. We all sense the power of this problem, even if we only see the tip of the iceberg. Yet even as our intoxication draws us away from our Maker and His mission, we're not sure what to do with it.

There's an obvious catch right off the bat: How could someone address the problem without promoting themselves at the same time? Who's going to listen to someone talk about our need for humility while simultaneously posing for pictures and expanding their platform with speaking tours and book signings? And even if someone *did* find a way to take themselves out of the spotlight, who would want to "waste" so much time and energy on a message that promised little to no credit? That would be taking it a little too far, right?

Truthfully, that's right where I was. I saw the problem but didn't know how to address it without winning the World's Biggest Hypocrite award. So, like many others, I just chose to ignore the issue altogether (along with all the implications it held on my own life).

I wanted to let go of this message, but—not unlike Jonah—God wouldn't let go of me.

Choosing to remain anonymous is not some ploy or gimmick to generate book sales. Trust me—this message has decimated my career ambitions! Since its unlikely inception, *Embracing Obscurity* has been from God and dedicated back to God. Still, I'm sure some skeptics will wonder if this is all a hoax. Others might question why I would use "Anonymous" as a byline yet use personal pronouns and my own stories and experiences.[1] I can only answer that I've come to realize embracing obscurity is not about wiping ourselves from existence but rather, voluntarily, becoming nothing in light of everything God is and has promised us. Why? So we can bring Him greater glory. It's about making Him, not ourselves, look good. Maybe in sharing some of the history behind *Embracing Obscurity*, I can lend credibility to my sincerity . . .

It all started one nondescript Sunday, as I sat listening to a guest preacher talk on the humility of Christ. He spoke of servanthood versus acts of service, of our puny attempts to "be somebody," and of a God who had everything yet chose to be nothing. As the Spirit moved, I was cut to the heart by his message. If any of us dare follow our suffering Servant-King, we must learn both to trust Him and to travel in His footsteps. My mind searched for a word to encompass all that was turning my world upside down. Then in a rare divine moment, the phrase came: *embrace obscurity.*

For a moment I was satisfied, kind of like finally remembering the words to a song you've been humming all day. Then the weight of the words began to sink in. *Wait . . . embrace obscurity? Who in their right mind would want to do that? And what would that do to my life?* But no matter how much I resisted the implications, I knew—right then and there—I must.

So began a journey—a sometimes painful journey—into the depth of Christ's humility. As I traveled (though I am far from arriving), I increasingly realized that this is a message not just for me, but for every follower of Christ—the comedian, the politician, the single mom, the bank teller, the CEO.

And I began to feel that God was asking me to share this message, which brought about the great quandary mentioned earlier: Even on my cleverest day, how could I justify the hypocrisy of writing—and taking credit for—a book called *Embracing Obscurity*?

Yet God wouldn't let it alone.

After some divine arm-twisting, *Embracing Obscurity*—and anonymity—was born. Apart from the surprisingly difficult logistics of writing anonymously (like keeping my own family in the dark), my flesh has been as rebellious as Terrell Owens at a press conference. Old sin dies hard. I've found myself imagining scenarios in which I get some sort of glory for the work involved in these pages: "accidental" discoveries, best-sellers' lists—even one daydream in which I was discovered by a respected mentor and rewarded on my deathbed. My pride evidently knows no bounds. The struggles I've encountered in writing this book have been poignant reminders that we all—myself included—need this message.

The church (again, including me) has come so far in imitating the world's tenets of success that we can barely distinguish the two. There's a sense of urgency in our condition I think few of us realize. And unless we find the antidote soon, we'll live and die in our self-deception. The urgency of this message compels me to pen these pages.

In the chapters ahead I'll try to keep to the background, letting Christ do His own work in your heart and life. As you read, and for the rest of your life, I pray that you will find and embrace the unsurpassable joy, freedom, and newfound purpose to be had in embracing obscurity.

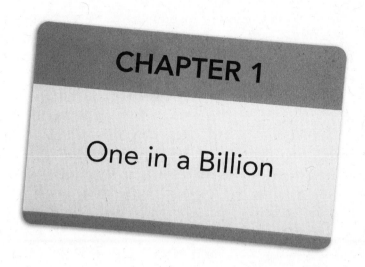

CHAPTER 1

One in a Billion

We are here for only a moment, visitors and
strangers in the land as our ancestors were before us.
Our days on earth are like a passing shadow,
gone so soon without a trace.

1 CHRONICLES 29:15 (NLT)

Our days on earth are like grass;
like wildflowers, we bloom and die.
As for man, his days are like grass—
he blooms like a flower of the field;
when the wind passes over it, it vanishes,
and its place is no longer known.

PSALM 103:15–16

Seven billion, twenty-five million, four hundred twenty
thousand, three hundred ninety.

That's our best guess at the number of people on planet Earth as I write this.[1] Hardly fodder for self-importance. But as the reality of numbers like that have a way of escaping us, if you really want your own insignificance to stare you in the face, try standing on top of the Empire State Building in New York City, while 8.3 million people sprawl out below. Attend a concert at the Northwest's Gorge Amphitheater, with twenty thousand people groovin' all around you. Take a long walk along the streets of Monaco, where thirty-three thousand people are crammed into less than a square mile. If you've ever gone to Disneyland in June, Mall of America in December, or tried to grab a hot deal on Black Friday, you know what I'm talking about. There are hoards of people on this planet.

Perhaps you, like me, can point to a specific instance when your self-important naiveté came crashing down. It was near 3:30 on a Friday afternoon, and I had the unfortunate need to be driving on a ridiculously crowded interstate. Stop-and-go traffic would have been preferable—we were just stopped dead. The cars across the median were lumbering along (lucky for them), and, since I had nothing better to do, I started watching weary commuters as they passed—a visibly agitated woman in a silk blouse applying lipstick; a Justin Timberlake look-alike in a newly polished Camaro, talking on his cell phone; a thirty-something singing like nobody's business; an older Asian lady in a supermarket uniform; a mom and her kids arguing; and they just kept coming . . . and coming . . . and coming.

After a hundred or so cars, I started to get a little depressed. Each one of these people had a life, a circle of acquaintances and family, a story to tell of their history, aspirations, disappointments, and fears. Who did I think I was, anyway, completely preoccupied with how this traffic jam was going to make me late for I-can't-even-remember-what? What could possibly possess me—or any of us—to think that my story, my *life*, is somehow different, unique, important?

Have you ever had one of these moments? A split second when the enormity of humanity pounds you into a pea-sized lump of insignificance? An occasion when a crowd leaves you feeling a little disillusioned and more than a little irrelevant? If not, look for one. As uncomfortable as is the prospect, unimportance is good for the soul.

Solomon got it. At first glance, his book Ecclesiastes is a real downer, especially to the world's optimists.

> "Everything is meaningless," says the Teacher, "completely meaningless!"
>
> What do people get for all their hard work under the sun? Generations come and generations go, but the earth never changes. The sun rises and the sun sets, then hurries around to rise again. The wind blows south, and then turns north. Around and around it goes, blowing in circles. Rivers run into the sea, but the sea is never full. Then the water returns again to the rivers and flows out again to the sea. Everything is wearisome beyond description. No matter how much we see, we are never satisfied. No matter how much we hear, we are not content.
>
> History merely repeats itself. It has all been done before. Nothing under the sun is truly new. Sometimes people say, "Here is something new!" But actually it is old; nothing is ever truly new. *We don't remember what happened in the past, and in future generations, no one will remember what we are doing now.* (Eccles. 1:2–11 NLT, emphasis added)

I told you it was a downer!

But wait, there's more. If nearly seven billion fellow humans coupled with the cyclical pattern of history have never underscored your unimportance, just look underfoot.

It's a Big, Big World

God spared no attention to detail or sheer quantity when creating *billions* of species no human being will ever even see. Science has done their best to name, categorize, describe, and study all the creepy crawlies, fungi, bacteria, and other strange organisms that live on and under the soil; but they readily admit there is no way to get to them all. Specialists estimate the number of fungi species likely reaches 1.5 million; and even though tens of thousands of roundworm types are already known, there are likely millions more completely undiscovered. The next time you shake the soil out of your garden gloves, imagine the millions of bacteria that live in just a gram of dirt, representing several *thousand* species.[2]

But if the sheer quantity of living things that live and die with no thought to our existence doesn't point you to something completely outside yourself, have you considered the universe lately?

When God created the heavens and Earth, He spared no expense. In fact, the vastness of the former borders on excess. Earth itself is impressive enough, with its precision orbit, delicately balanced atmosphere, laws of nature and physics, varied life forms, and intricate biodiversity. But Earth is minuscule in size and influence when compared with the grandeur of the heavens.

If our solar system were represented on a twelve-inch ruler, our sun (which is more than one hundred times the diameter of Earth) would be smaller than the period at the end of this sentence. On this same scale, our galaxy, The Milky Way, would be larger than the Pacific Ocean. But we're not done yet. If you could zoom out even farther, you would see that God has created an innumerable number of galaxies. Innumerable! Our own galaxy is home to more than one hundred billion stars, let alone multiplying that by infinity.[3]

This realization should bring new meaning to Psalm 147:4, "He counts the number of the stars; He gives names to all of them." Isaiah 40:26 says, "Look up and see: who created these? He brings out the starry host by number; He calls all of them by name. Because of His great power and strength, not one of them is missing." And yet we are told all this is "but the fringes of His ways; how faint is the word we hear of Him! Who can understand His mighty thunder?" (Job 26:14).

Feeling small yet?

If so, you're in good company. Many faithful men and women have come to think little of themselves in light of all that God is and does. As Thomas à Kempis said:

> He who would learn to serve must first learn to think little of himself. This is the highest and most profitable lesson, truly to know and to despise ourselves. To have no opinion of ourselves—and to think always well and highly of others is great wisdom and perfection.[4]

We like the thought of "perfection." We can tolerate the idea of "thinking well and highly of others." So why are we turned off by this "highest and most profitable lesson"—to think little of ourselves?

The Nature of Obscurity

The trouble with you and me and the rest of humanity is not that we lack self-confidence (as we're told by the world) but that we have far too much self-importance. The thought of being just another of the roughly one hundred billion people to have ever graced this planet offends us—whether we realize it or not. We have such a high opinion of ourselves that to live and die unnoticed seems a grave injustice. Yet for the vast majority of us, has God called us to anything else? *Webster's* defines *obscurity* as, "relatively unknown: as . . . (b) not prominent or famous."[5] That pretty much sums up the vast majority of humankind, doesn't it? Even those rare men and women who make a mark on our society—a passionate speaker, a star athlete, an active politician, a gifted musician, an empathetic humanitarian—they're still "relatively unknown" in the grand scope of the world's consciousness and especially in light of history. Even we authors can't escape obscurity. Every time I visit a Barnes & Noble, I'm ready to lay down my pen for good. Solomon's words taunt me as I stare at the obscene number of volumes: "There is no end to the making of many books" (Eccles. 12:12)!

In the big picture we're all in this obscurity thing together. That's hard to remember in our little bubbles of influence. It's easy to think we're somebody when we're well known at church, or in a particular industry, or at our children's schools. When we have a nice portfolio, or a few letters after our name, or have a commemorative plaque on a little park bench somewhere, our pride creeps in and tempts us to want more: more recognition, more admiration, more influence, more, more, more. Few, myself included, have ever given thought to wanting less.

Obscurity comes in two forms: It can be either assigned (by God) or chosen (by us). I don't know whether one is harder than the other. I just know that from a prideful, human point of view, either can gnaw at us. We don't want to live as one in a crowd. We don't want to be just another person living in a subdivision in the suburban sprawl that has become America. And we certainly don't want to die without making our mark on something . . . *anything*.

A handful of truly "great" people on this planet will become immortal in the history books as world-changers. But since there's little chance the likes of them will ever have cause to read yours truly, I can effectively ignore that group for now. For the rest of us, the 99.9 percent of humankind that fall into the first category, our lot of obscurity has been assigned. As much as we claw and clamor, whine and pout, we're just not going to be an Alexander the Great, a Queen Elizabeth, or even a Mother Teresa or a Billy Graham.

Even when an overarching, global obscurity has been assigned to us, we still have a choice of whether to embrace *personal* obscurity—an obscurity of heart as much as position. And *that* is the message I believe God has for us, a message He modeled as well as taught.

An Obscure Sacrifice

We hear all the time about the Bible's "great men and women," the real "heroes of the faith." But I wonder if all their notability has not come from being made immortal in a document that has been read the world over. Think about it: If the lives and deaths of Joseph, Rachel, Jonah, Abraham, Moses, Nehemiah, even King David or the apostle Paul had not been divinely recorded in the pages of our Bibles, would we have any idea in the twenty-first century who they were? No more than other faithful men, women, and martyrs of ancient and modern civilizations who now lie nameless in the dust. Being of great faith does not guarantee timeless notoriety. Take as exhibit A "the young boy" of loaves and fishes fame.

You are likely familiar with Jesus' miracle of feeding the five thousand. The Sunday school version goes something like this: As Jesus was teaching and healing a large crowd one day, it got to be late—too late to go home for dinner, and people (including the disciples) were starting to get a little cranky from their hunger. Of course, no one wanted to go home and risk missing any of what Jesus had to say. Enter "young boy." Jesus strangely asks Philip where they could buy bread to feed such a large crowd of people. Andrew says sarcastically, "Hey, there's a kid here with a few chunks of bread and a couple of dried fish. Ha-ha. But what are we going to do with that?" Of course Jesus knew exactly what He was going to do with that boy's lunch. He had known all day. He had known His whole life. He was going to feed thousands.

Now think with me about this kid for a minute. He not only has the maturity to be spending his Saturday listening to a sermon rather than hanging out at the skate park, but he also had the remarkable faith to hand over the only food he had *with no promise of return*. Who knows—maybe he was a little miffed at giving up his eats. But since I doubt the disciples manhandled the kid to take his lunch from him, he must have given it willingly in the end. And just like the son who whined and pouted but still did what his father asked (see Matt. 21:28–32), this kid got full credit for obedience, even if his heart wasn't *completely* in the right place at first. (Comforting thought, isn't it? Which of us doesn't have our own attitude issues?) Whatever his initial response, I'd say his act of surrender took remarkable faith! Yet in none of the Gospels are we even given his name, and he is never mentioned again.

Have you ever been asked this small-group ice-breaker question, "What Bible story character would you like to be?" Would this be yours? Would you want to be "the young boy"? Would you be willing to remain nameless, offering up your meager portion to your Savior, with no promise of return or guarantee of notoriety, but in complete obedience allow God to work His miracle through your small "lunch"? That's what embracing obscurity is all about: being content with being "relatively unknown" so that Christ can be made more known. Temporarily going hungry so that many more may be filled.

I want to close this chapter with a passage that will become familiar over the next ten chapters. As you read these words, marvel at the majesty and splendor of a God who could create innumerable species with a word, a God who knows trillions of stars by name yet would choose to become "relatively unknown" for your sake and mine.

> Make your own attitude that of Christ Jesus, who, existing in the form of God, did not consider equality with God as something to be used for His own advantage. Instead He emptied Himself by assuming the form of a slave, taking on the likeness of men. And when He had come as a man in His external form, He humbled Himself by becoming obedient to the point of death—even to death on a cross. For this reason God highly exalted Him and gave Him the name that is above every name, so that at the name of Jesus every knee should bow—of those who are in heaven and on

earth and under the earth—and every tongue should confess that Jesus Christ is Lord, to the glory of God the Father. (Phil. 2:5–10)

Discussion Questions

1. Have you ever had an experience that made you feel insignificant in light of the sheer number of people on this planet? An occasion when a crowd left *you* feeling a bit irrelevant?

2. Do you think our culture encourages people to feel important? If so, how?

3. Would you describe most of the people you know as generally lacking self-confidence or having too much self-importance?

4. What experiences here on Earth remind you most of God's vastness? What reminds you most of His attention to detail?

5. Do you agree that, "In the big picture we're all in this obscurity thing together"? Does the idea of obscurity in this life sit well with you?

6. If the idea of embracing your own obscurity rubs you wrong, what do you think are the root causes of those feelings? What beliefs, past experiences, or current circumstances might be contributing to your reluctance?

7. How would you describe the difference between an obscurity of *position* and an obscurity of *heart*? Do you find the thought of one to be easier to swallow than the other?

8. If embracing obscurity hinges on "being content with being 'relatively unknown' so that Christ can be made more known," how might Christ be made more known through your own obscurity?

CHAPTER 2

Embracing Definition

We are all motivated by a keen desire for praise.

CICERO

*I'm not asking that you take [my people]
out of the world, but that you guard them
from the Evil One. They are no more defined
by the world than I am defined by the world.*

JOHN 17:15–16 (THE MESSAGE)

My right index finger paused midair, frozen in indecision. Should I click the mouse or forget I had ever felt convicted for wasting monumental amounts of my time? My hesitation to follow through with this simple click was absurd to me, even in the moment. This wasn't a life-or-death decision. Not even close. So why couldn't I just *do* it?

I had toyed with the thought of "unplugging" from social networking websites for a few months. I was disturbed—yes, at times disgusted—by how much time was siphoned away by keeping up with "friends" (many of whom, I might add, I hadn't missed talking to in fifteen years but now, suddenly, couldn't bear to part with). My frustration with my own lack of discipline, and the realization that I had ultimately let these sites become a form of—dare I say—web sin, finally came to a head. I knew what I had to do. But would I do it?

The morning of Facebook D-day, I started the process as I often approach obedience—completely halfheartedly. Rather than just delete my account, I first tried whittling down my friends list. Another monumental waste of time. Took half a day to "unfriend" a hundred people, at which point I realized that I could possibly waste yet another week of my life trying to decide who should go and who should stay. So I made the jump, and nervously clicked on my account settings.

In the ten minutes that followed, I began to see the unveiling of Facebook's grip on the world, not unlike Dorothy's discovery that the wizard of Oz was all smoke and mirrors. In my quest to close my account, I was funneled through a maze of tricks to get me to stay. *Are you sure you want to do this?* it asked. *What are your reasons for leaving? Worried about your privacy? No problem. Just enable more privacy settings. Spending too much time on Facebook? We can fix that too.* The blows kept hitting lower. The next screen opened several pictures of those I had talked to most since opening my account. *But if you leave, Granny will miss you. Your own father will miss you. Your children will no longer know you exist. How* could *you leave them now?*

That's where I sat, my finger poised over the mouse, contemplating the decision before me. I'm happy (though slightly embarrassed) to say that after another twenty minutes sitting at that computer, I did it. I clicked the final button, and the aftermath was completely and humiliatingly anticlimactic. The final page came up on the screen: *No biggie. If you ever want to come back, just sign in to reactivate your account.* What? Sign right back in? You mean to tell me that after all that, I don't even get the satisfaction of finality? I think I was hoping they'd be mad or something. Hurt. Maybe even some virtual tears. Heartbroken to see me go would have been a little more rewarding, considering the tremendous internal battle I had been waging for months over the decision. But the nonchalance of Facebook's final good-bye forced me to see how insignificant my presence on the website really was.

The repercussions of my decision to unplug from social media had a much more profound affect on me than I had anticipated. After a few days I caught myself wondering if anyone (other than Granny, Dad, and my children) even knew I was "gone." I also came to realize that I had actually let triple-digit "friends" become a status. I had taken pride in getting responses to witty things I'd post or compliments from long-lost acquaintances about my beautiful family or my relative "success" in life. Once again I saw that the depth of my pride knows no bounds. And in the months since that experience, I've been chewing on this question: *What else do we allow to define us?*

Bookstores and Subtitles

In the world of publishing, everyone's out to make a buck. That's even true of most Christian publishers. I'm not raging against the machine here, just stating the facts. Of course, it makes sense when you think about it. Who's going to stay in business publishing books that no one will buy? No matter how clever, colloquial, or convicting a manuscript is, if it's not going to sell, you can't publish it. Bills trump philanthropy (almost) every time. The job, then, of an acquisitions team (the people who choose which books to print), is to weed out the unsellable stuff and find those gems that are marketable to the broadest audiences.

Here's another piece of commonsense trivia: Contrary to your mother's assurances, the general public *does* in fact judge books by their covers, at least when they enter a Barnes & Noble or Family Christian Store. Haven't you? But what exactly are we looking for? What catches our eye? All those beautiful paperbacks or hardcover editions are wrapped in three important things: the design, the author's name, and the title. The cover design is up to the graphics team, so an acquisitions editor is looking for two things: a popular name and an intriguing title. Either will do nicely to secure a second look from Joe or Jane shopper.

In the big bookstore of life, you and I don't operate much differently. We know that others are judging us by our "cover," and we really, *really* want them to like what they see. We want them to take a second look. Why? Maybe we're after their respect or admiration. Perhaps we have an unhealthy "fear of man" (Prov. 29:25). Maybe, if we're honest, we wouldn't mind if the person on the other end was just a *tad* bit jealous of us. A low self-esteem, topsy-turvy priorities, or selfish ambition might play a part. Our personal motivations are likely a unique smattering of our own personal junk. Whatever our reasoning, if we don't have as much control over the "cover art" (our outward appearance) as we'd like, we have to make sure we seal the deal with either an impressive name or a flashy subtitle.

Does your name raise eyebrows by itself, or does it need a little extra oomph? Unless you're a Justin Bieber, Shania

Twain, or Brett Favre, your name alone might not have the respect-securing effect we're all after. In an attempt to be a somebody, have you—like me and so many others—adopted an impressive subtitle?

Not sure? Well, what's the one thing you're tempted to bring up in the course of conversation when establishing your identity for the first time? When you want to impress someone? It might be as short as, "I'm Jenny, the VP of marketing and a working mom," or, "Hey, I'm Kyle, and I just produced my first movie." Your subtitle might be short and simple, or it might be akin to the 227-word "full style" of the sultans of the Ottoman Empire—like "Suleiman I, His Imperial Majesty Grand Sultan, Commander of the Faithful and Successor of the Prophet of the Lord of the Universe," *for short.* (Of course, you or I would *never* be so vain . . . right?)

But, seriously, what is it for you? I sure know my subtitles of choice. They've changed over the years to account for the different roles I've held and jobs I've done. But to be honest, they've all been about one thing: *me.* Even weaving ministry credentials in there doesn't mask the underlying desire to make others think I'm a somebody. That I matter. That I'm going places. I'm itching for admiration, respect, and yes, even jealousy. It's ugly and it's wrong, but I'm just being honest here.

Sometimes we see our own sin more clearly when we first view it in someone else. For whatever reason, hearing another person's story can often help us make sense of our own. With that in mind, I'd like to introduce you to a few folks I've gotten to know over the years. These are all individuals I have known or have interviewed in the past about what it looks like to rally for admiration, recognition, or fame in real-world contexts. I think you'll see, however, that when our hearts are laid bare, any one of us could be "exhibit A." Perhaps as you hear the stories of these average men and women, you'll find a fresh view of your own hidden motivations.

Keep in mind, not all subtitles point to an accomplishment, but all point to a pursuit, and the end goal is looking good in others' eyes.

Zac Taylor: Outdoor Adventurer

Zac's pride is as difficult for others to detect as it is for him to see, largely because he truly couldn't care less about the contemporary standard of success: education, job, money, etc. He works so he can play, making just enough money to fund the next backpacking trip, island getaway, safari, or dive.

It's just this laissez-faire attitude about life that has inadvertently allowed pride to waltz in through the back door. At first Zac genuinely didn't care what others thought about his life choices, but once he noticed that others admired him for his carefree style and adrenaline-seeking adventures, he was only more drawn to pursue those things. Now his identity is so wrapped up in this image he has created that the thought of being "just another guy," with a desk job and a family to take care of, scares him.

Chase Brooks: Up and Coming Exec

Toward the end of high school, Chase decided he wanted to become a pastor. But when he told his parents the news, they flipped. They said he needed to go to college and get a "real job," so he did.

Following his parents' advice, Chase earned a masters in business finance and did, in fact, land a job that paid well. Within his field he's well known and well liked. He's considered an "expert" at what he does, and others respect him. He can afford to buy his wife and daughter nice things and owns a gorgeous home in an expensive area.

Chase still loves the Lord. He's committed to his church and is glad his income enables him to give generously to others. But he's beginning to realize that pride took root a long time ago and has been slowly growing ever since. The litmus test? If Chase's vocation were taken from him and he was forced to work in a lesser-known capacity, losing the comforts of recognition and wealth, he would feel an incredible loss of identity. Over time he has allowed success in his field to define his success as a person.

Megan Keller: Your New Best Friend

Our subtitles don't only develop from a profession or lack thereof. Megan would admit to you that she takes most pride in being everyone's friend. If someone doesn't like her right off the bat, she gets a little self-conscious. She works hard to make sure that she's likable, and likable she is. Megan is one of those people who puts you at ease right away. She can relate to just about anybody or anything, adapting to the people around her like a chameleon.

Of course, making others feel important and appreciated can be a healthy by-product of humility. But at the heart of the matter, Megan's ultimate motivation is not others-focused but self-focused. She has come to define her success as a person by the success of her relationships—by whether people like her, want to be near her, or want to be her friend.

Dan Perkins: Pastor of a Large Church

If asked whether Dan takes pride in being a pastor, he'd reply, "Absolutely." And his pride is not all unfounded. The apostle Paul rightfully boasted that he and his companions had invested themselves in kingdom work, "in simplicity and godly sincerity, not with fleshly wisdom but by the grace of God, and more abundantly toward you" (2 Cor. 1:12 NKJV). Paul took pride in Christ, and he knew there is a sense in which those committed to living a Christlike lifestyle (which is not, by the way, limited to traditional or formal ministry) might take pride in the sacrifice because he knew that anything good in us is Christ (see Gal. 2:20). But this is not, unfortunately, the case for Dan.

Pastor Dan planted his church in a largely unchurched area and watched the congregation grow from two to nearly two thousand over ten years. As much as he publicly credits God for that growth, Dan has been heard privately attributing his own speaking ability, leadership skills, or even his "great" faith, for the increase. If the church were to fold in a year, Dan would be devastated. His success as a person—and in this case, as a believer—is interwoven into the success of "his" church.

Lillian Daniels: Creative Working Mom

Lilly would confess that her subtitle's "full style" would include a few other things, including "fun and creative friend," "mom of the year," and "completely balanced life." She wants to do and be it all.

Lilly doesn't have the option of not working, but because she is able to care for her children by running a small business out of her home, she meets the admiration, and occasional jealousy, of other working moms. And, truthfully, she wouldn't necessarily want to be "just" a mom, even if she could. This quote, cut out from a magazine, hangs on her fridge:

You wear many hats. And while I get that the weight of all those hats can wear you down, at least be happy you've got something important to do.

The got-it-all-together exterior melts down occasionally, however, to reveal some hidden motivations. Every once in a while she feels this nagging sense of lacking, and she worries that she's not the awesome person she's trying to portray to herself and others. In those moments she feels like she hasn't accomplished enough.

Matt Cooper: Aspiring Pro

Matt is a young athlete who epitomizes the "pro" dream: wanting to make a living doing something really cool. Though he plays football, Matt's story echos that of many a musician, dancer, surfer, magician, and ultimate fighter. His passionate desire to pursue his talent is equally matched by other, less-desirable motivations.

If asked why he wants to "go pro," Matt would tell you he loves playing the game, but in more introspective conversations he can't deny the importance of others' admiration for what he does or will do. Money, fame, respect, and validation are a few other driving forces behind Matt's goals. He can't wait to prove the "doubters" wrong by making it big—by *proving* himself.

Jenny Austin: Christian Writer/Speaker

An author and speaker at women's events, Jenny Austin spends much of her life studying and teaching the Bible. From outward appearances you might think this gracious woman couldn't possibly struggle with pride, but her candid feelings prove that none of us are immune:

I love what I do—until I walk into a library and see thousands of neglected volumes collecting dust, or hear about yet another big speakers' conference where dozens of women will be sharpening their skills to do just what I do, and possibly better.

Being faced with the relative commonality of her skills reveals a side to Jenny that worries her.

I've always thought that I was humbly presenting the Word of Truth to others because it's an irresistible calling on my life, but recently I've been questioning what my true motivations are. Have I let 'success' go to my head? It's so hard to remove myself from the equation when others admire me for my—even spiritual—accomplishments.

Maria Oliver: The Pretty Girl

Remember, not all subtitles point to an accomplishment, but all point to a pursuit. Maria's pursuit is the flighty ideal of one of society's most fickle idols: beauty. Now don't assume she's the plastic-surgery cover model you see on the covers of magazines at the check-out line at Walmart. Maria is a beautiful woman, perhaps uncommonly beautiful, but she's still a normal gal. You'd never know how concerned she is with her appearance.

Maria did poorly in school, but she says she learned fast that pretty girls don't have to be smart. She got all the positive attention she craved just by looking good. So she got obsessed with clothes, makeup, and pulling together a photo-finish look each day. All these years later she still struggles with wanting others to think she's pretty when they first meet her. Even though it sounds "sick," she says, she wants others to be jealous of how she looks so that it won't matter what she's done or what she's accomplished.

Pride takes all forms, doesn't it?

So I ask again, *What's your subtitle?* Obviously, these examples don't cover every single subtitle we create for ourselves. Yours might be completely different or a mixture of a few. If you're having trouble putting your finger on your subtitle, the following questions might help. As you read through them, reflect on your own story and the motivations behind it.

- When you meet someone for the first time, what is the first or most important thing you want that person to know about who you are, what you do, or what you have done?
- If you lost your current vocation (not just your current position) and were forced to work in a lesser-known capacity (think: Discovery's *Dirty Jobs*), would you feel a sense of loss or a change in your identity?
- On a scale of 1 to 10, how important is it to you that others admire you for what you do or have done in life? (1=not at all important, 10=very important)
- How is "success" defined in your genre of work or performance? In other words, what would it look like for someone to "make it" in your field? Is it your goal to "make it"? If not, what is your goal (if any)?
- On a scale of 1 to 10, what role does success (as you define it) play in whether you feel you are all-around "successful" as a person? (1=doesn't factor in, 10=they're practically synonymous)
- Do you tie your identity to any other relationships in your life? (e.g., a popular boyfriend? a gorgeous wife? a star-athlete son or daughter?)

- If you have left a career/vocation to be a stay-at-home parent, do you feel a sense of loss of identity? What thoughts or emotions come into play when someone asks you what you "do"?
- If you were able to quit your job tomorrow and be a stay-at-home parent, would you do it? How do you expect you would feel? Would you perceive any loss of identity?

Strangling Embrace

At first our self-promoting subtitles might make us feel all snug and secure, like a cozy blanket wrapped around our shoulders on a cold day. But the nature of pride is, of course, much more sinister and even deadly. More like an anaconda than a fuzzy blanket, pride continues to tighten its death grip, eventually choking out all humility and ending in our complete consumption with self.

Reminds me of another snake . . . another story of pride.

It's interesting (at the very least) that Satan was cast down from heaven because of his pride, then tried to trick Eve into the sin of pride by appealing to her pride. Satan could have used any number of approaches in trying to get her to disobey God's command to let that fruit be, but having been undone by his own ego, I guess he figured that his best shot was to go for the tried and true. *After all,* he might have reasoned, *if I fell for it—I who am the greatest—who wouldn't?* So he appealed to Eve's desire to be great:

"'No! You will not die," the serpent said to the woman. "In fact, God knows that when you eat it your eyes will be opened and you will be like God, knowing good and evil.'"(Gen. 3:4–5)

And she bought it, hook, line, and sinker.

"Then the woman saw that the tree was good for food and delightful to look at, and that it was desirable for obtaining wisdom. So she took some of its fruit and ate it." (v. 6)

It was the sin that was Satan's undoing, and ours. Ever since that day in the garden, mankind has battled with pride. Sadly, those who follow Christ are no exception.

Pride is one of the last holdouts as the Spirit transforms the believer, crucifying our flesh and uniting our hearts with Christ. Of course, it *will* go, once and for all (praise God!), when we are raised through Christ into immortality. But if we are to submit our lives to God in this life, allowing Him to dictate the course of our pursuits, we must wage a continual battle. His Word is clear on the matter.

The following verses may be familiar to you. Familiar passages are, unfortunately, prone to get glanced over. Before you read the following, take a few moments to prepare your heart and mind to read them afresh. Ask God to open your eyes to correlations between your own pride (rather than hypothetical pride or someone else's pride) and any unhealthy subtitles you have developed, or pursuits you have allowed to define you, in whole or in part.

All who fear the LORD will hate evil. Therefore, I hate pride and arrogance, corruption and perverse speech. (Prov. 8:13 NLT)

When pride comes, disgrace follows, but with humility comes wisdom. (Prov. 11:2)

The reflections of the heart belong to man, but the answer of the tongue is from the LORD. All a man's ways seem right in his own eyes, but the LORD weighs the motives. Commit your activities to the LORD and your plans will be achieved. (Prov. 16:1–3)

Everyone with a proud heart is detestable to the LORD; be assured, he will not go unpunished. (Prov. 16:5)

Pride comes before destruction, and an arrogant spirit before a fall. Better to be lowly of spirit with the humble than to divide plunder with the proud. (Prov. 16:18–19)

His ego is inflated; he is without integrity. But the righteous one will live by his faith. . . . An arrogant man is never at rest. (Hab. 2:4–5)

He told them, "Whoever welcomes this little child in My name welcomes Me. And whoever welcomes Me welcomes Him who sent Me. For whoever is least among you—this one is great." (Luke 9:48)

But when you are invited, go and recline in the lowest place, so that when the one who invited you comes, he will say to you, "Friend, move up higher." You will then be honored in the presence of all the other guests. For everyone who exalts himself will be humbled, and the one who humbles himself will be exalted. (Luke 14:10–11)

But it must not be like [the world] among you. On the contrary, whoever is greatest among you must become like the youngest, and whoever leads, like the one serving. For who is greater, the one at the table or the one serving? Isn't it the one at the table? But I am among you as the One who serves. (Luke 22:26–27)

But He gives greater grace. Therefore He says: "God resists the proud, but gives grace to the humble." (James 4:6)

Come now, you who say, "Today or tomorrow we will travel to such and such a city and spend a year there and do business and make a profit." You don't even know what tomorrow will bring—what your life will be! For you are a bit of smoke that appears for a little while, then vanishes. Instead, you should say, "If the Lord wills, we will live and do this or that." But as it is, you boast in your arrogance. All such boasting is evil. So it is a sin for the person who knows to do what is good and doesn't do it." (James 4:13–17)

A Different Embrace

By Christ's own decree, we should be no more defined by the world than He is. Ours should be a different embrace.

The depth of my own pride is seemingly infinite. Every time I think it's under wraps, I find some new variety of this cancerous sin hiding out in the darker corners of my heart. And not unlike cancer, what I think is full recovery from pride is oftentimes only remission. Given the right conditions—perhaps a bit of success, a dash of praise, a flattering "friend," or a lack of accountability—the cancer returns. It keeps showing up in one form or another. We need to take drastic measures if we're going to do serious battle against this deep-rooted sin.

So what should we do once we discover pride in our lives? How do we break free from its embrace? The answer is two-fold. First, we have to admit that we *can't* do it in our own strength. You'll recall that wanting to be like God—complete with omnipotence and perfection—is what landed us in this mess in the first place. Rather, we have to submit ourselves to the One who humbled Himself to the point of death to rescue us from our self-righteousness and sin.

Second, we have to follow His example by heeding God's instructions. The earthly antidote to pride, just like every other sin, is found in Scripture. Let's recap the verses we just read. According to those verses, if we want to ditch our pride we must:

- Fear the Lord (Prov. 8:13).
- Embrace wisdom (Prov. 11:2).
- Commit our actions to the Lord (Prov. 16:1–3).
- Live humbly and do right (Prov. 16:18–19).
- Don't trust ourselves; live by faithfulness to God (Hab. 2:4).
- Associate with the lowly, for Christ's sake. Strive to be least (Luke 9:48).

- Humble ourselves by settling for less than we "deserve" (Luke 14:10–11).
- Serve others (Luke 22:26–27).
- Receive God's grace to stand against evil desires (James 4:6).
- Don't boast about our plans, but submit them to the Lord (James 4:13–17).

Easy to read, much harder to digest and apply! Perhaps that's why my heart really and truly rejoices when I hear of men and women who understand the seriousness of this disease and choose to deal with it accordingly. Rather than play it down, these saints take action.

I recently read of a pastor who was determined to be defined by a different embrace. This well-known speaker, author, and pastor stepped back from ministry when he realized just how deep pride had taken root in his heart. This is an excerpt from the letter he wrote to his congregation to explain his upcoming eight-month leave of absence:

> I see several species of pride in my soul that, while they may not rise to the level of disqualifying me for ministry, grieve me, and have taken a toll on my relationship with [my wife] and others who are dear to me. How do I apologize to you, not for a specific deed, but for ongoing character flaws, and their effects on everybody? I'll say it now, and no doubt will say it again, I'm sorry. Since I don't have just one deed to point to, I simply ask for a spirit of forgiveness; and I give you as much assurance as I can that I am not making peace, but war, with my own sins. . . . In 30 years, I have never let go of the passion for public productivity. In this leave,

I intend to let go of all of it. . . . It would be just like God to do the greatest things when I am not there."[1]

That's the type of tenacity we need in order to gut pride from our lives.

Once we discover our pride, to ignore it means certain death—in a very spiritual, and in some cases eternal, sense.

What have you allowed to define you? What role has pride played in your pursuits? These are not easy questions but must be answered, as we'll see, if you desire to take on the disposition of Christ.

Discussion Questions

1. A "subtitle" is something we allow to define us, and that we want others to know about us. So, *what's your subtitle*? (If you're not sure, look again at the list of questions on pages 27–28.)

- Subtitle 1—
- Subtitle 2—
- Subtitle 3—

2. When you share your subtitle with someone, what response are you *really* hoping for? Admiration? Respect? Jealousy?

3. To which of the eight "real life" examples of subtitles in this chapter do you relate most?

4. Are you surprised by the correlation between the subtitles you allow to define you and pride?

5. While the most important element in battling our pride is dependence on God's Spirit, Scripture also outlines some practical steps we must take. Look again at the list of commands on pages 32–33. Now give three practical steps you need to take to begin battling pride in your own life.

- Action Step 1—
- Action Step 2—
- Action Step 3—

CHAPTER 3

Embracing the Humble King

Make your own attitude that of Christ Jesus.

Without question, this is the great mystery of our faith:
Christ was revealed in a human body.

1 TIMOTHY 3:16 (NLT)

Did the earthly life of our Lord appear to be
a thundering success? Would the statistics of souls won,
crowds made into faithful disciples, sermons heeded,
commands obeyed, be impressive? Hardly.

ELISABETH ELLIOT[1]

lud • i • cra • thet • ic \\ˈlü-də-krə-ˈthe-tik\ *adj.* : A combination of ludicrous and apathetic, describing a state in which the divinely ridiculous has become so commonplace that it is no longer of special interest or compelling.

No, you won't find it in the dictionary, but I can't think of a better word to describe the way we have come to view the incarnation of Christ. Consider with me . . .

The Supreme Being; the One who spoke our entire universe into being with a word, yet cannot be bound by human language; the Namer of stars and the Crusher of mountains; the God whose face necessitates veiling to preserve a man's life; the one responsible for each breath you've taken while reading this paragraph; the only omniscient, omnipotent and omnipresent reality—yeah, *this* God—became a roughly eight-pound mass of created cells. He took on skin, blood, and DNA and all the pain, heartbreak, and weakness that go along with those trappings. He became *human*. The weakest form of human at that.

You really can't get any more helpless than an infant. If you've taken care of one, you recognize that his existence depends on another human being to keep him alive. He can't eat, take shelter, or keep from danger on his own. A baby's life depends completely on his or her caregiver's competence.

So there was Jesus—Son of the everlasting God as homosapien, relying on His mommy to nurse Him and change His diapers.

Ludicrathetic.

Seriously, how can the magnitude of this escape us? How can we get through a complete day without falling on our knees in awe of this truth? What keeps us numb to the jaw-dropping implications of Creator becoming creature?

I once heard of a robber who waltzed into a store in plain daylight, without any disguise, betting that no one would suspect a plainclothes patron of demanding money at gun-point. Though the criminal was eventually caught, he nearly pulled off an impressive heist on one principle: *Normalcy rarely stirs suspicion.*

I think this is what Satan is banking on, at least in Western civilization. Instead of squelching any mention of the most marvelous, divine event in Earth's history, he has allowed it to be (perhaps even nudged it?) front and center. *Why would he do that?* you might wonder. Because of the plainclothes robber principle. Ironically, it's hard *not* to get numb to the splendor of a God-Man when we have an entire, exhausting season to celebrate it—*every* year. We get lulled into thinking that we *are* keenly aware of this unlikely plan of God's to send His Son as a baby. After all, it's the reason for church musicals, gift exchanges, brightly lit trees, Christmas carol-a-thons, and festive sleigh rides through the snow. Even amid the blatant materialism of the season, the true message surrounds most of us for a good month out of every year. Thus, Satan hasn't had to do *anything* on his own to divert our full attention from marveling at the ridiculousness. Instead, he has allowed us to backhandedly keep ourselves from soaking in the glorious hope of the reality of Christ's birth by sanctioning an entire holiday season to do just that.

They don't call him deceiver for nothing.

What's also incredible to me, and sheds so much light into God's nature, is that He lets this all happen.

I try not to do much shopping in the mayhem of the holidays, but sometimes it's inevitable. On one such outing, a common sight struck me as rather peculiar. A traditional nativity scene sat on a shelf, under a large sign reading "25 percent off." I noted the usual attendees: Mary; Joseph; a couple shepherds; the chronologically and numerically inaccurate wise men; and in the center a Gerber baby-esque infant, looking bright eyed and cheerful lying in his unlikely crib. Right next to the nativity scene was an eight-inch jolly ol' Santa, rosy cheeked and seeming to look down on Jesus through his bifocals, as if to say, "Oh-ho, isn't He cute?"

I stared for a minute, until the subtle message sank in: The birth of our Lord reduced to discounted holiday ware, given the same shelf space as a fictional (and rather ridiculous) character! I quickly walked away, half envisioning a bolt of lightning blazing down from heaven to incinerate the blasphemy! But of course no bolt came, and that got me to thinking too. *What kind of God would allow His ludicrous act of mercy and salvation to become common fare at a discount store?*

An incredibly *humble* God.

Not weak, not ignorant, not even complacent or oblivious to the injustice. A *justly* and *graciously* humble God who manifests His humility not only in overlooking our profanity for a time but in sending His Son, Jesus Christ, in the first place. Jesus Christ, who:

> Existing in the form of God, did not consider equality with God as something to be used for His own advantage. Instead He emptied Himself by assuming the form of a slave, taking on the likeness of men. And when He had come as a man in His external form, He humbled Himself by becoming obedient to the point of death—even to death on a cross. (Phil. 2:6–8)

In an effort to counter our ludicratheticity (why not?), will you read that passage one more time? Savor the words. Let the implications sink deep into your soul.

Equality with God *not* something to take advantage of?
Emptied Himself of divine privileges?

Assumed the form of a *slave*?
Took on a human *body*?
Died a *brutal* and *unfair* death?
Are you *kidding* me?

As if becoming human wasn't debasing enough, He came as the most humble, least showy of men. Let's think about this rationally for a moment. If I were a god, and let's say I was a really merciful one, and I decided I was going to save humanity by becoming one of my creations (which I'd honestly never do to begin with), you bet your boots I'd be coming with some pomp and gusto. I'd be looking to show the world what a pure and loving sacrifice I was making for them. There would be armies at attention, parades in my honor, and—the actual death part?—I'd be humanely euthanized amid cheering crowds chanting my name.

Jesus' model of selfless service and obscure suffering doesn't jive with our subconscious ideas of what God-of-the-universe-turned-man should be. Humanly speaking, how much more likely would these candidates be for messiahship than "Mary and Joseph's kid"?

Alexander the Great—This self-proclaimed son of the gods had conquered most of the known world by the age of twenty-five. By the age of thirty-two (very close to Christ's age at the time of His death), Alexander had forged an empire unlike any the world had ever seen, or has seen since. Many consider him to be history's greatest conqueror.[2]

Muhammad—This guy is ranked first in *The 100: A Ranking of the World's Most Influential Persons in History*[3] because of his "supreme success" in both the religious and secular realms. He has influenced most of the world not only because he's the central human figure of Islam but because he was also active as a social reformer, diplomat, merchant, philosopher, orator, legislator, and military leader.

Brad Pitt—This well-known actor holds the world captive with good looks, charisma and the universal draw of philanthropy. In contrast to Jesus, who the Bible says had "nothing beautiful or majestic about his appearance, nothing to attract us to him" (Isa. 53:2 NLT), Brad seems to hold the backing of an entire class of people simply by being a two-time "Sexiest Man Alive" winner.

Any of these choices or, even better, a divine cocktail of history's best, would seem more logical. I mean, I'm only human, but even I could think up a mover and shaker with the brains of Aristotle, the physique of Samson, the fame of Michael Jackson, and the military might of Genghis Khan. Since God is supremely committed to the honor of His name (see Isa. 48:11; Ezek. 20:9), wouldn't a crowd-pleasing superstar make God's glory shine brightest? Why wouldn't God have gone that route?

Perhaps for the precise reason, once again, that normalcy rarely stirs suspicion.

Obviously, God was capable of building the finest Messiah-Machine imaginable. The bodily choice for His Son, then, should give us pause. The earthly circumstances in which God placed the Christ, the Promised One, the Redeemer, should be cause for reflection. Shall we?

A Small-Town Boy

When my oldest daughter was about three years old, she went through a phase when she would ask whoever was tucking her in to tell her a "fun memory" before the lights were turned out at bedtime. Occasionally she'd ask me to tell her about the day she was born. I'd tell her all the details of her birth day that I could remember, from the two-hour drive through mountain roads to the hospital, to her terminally ill grandmother making a four-hour trip to see her come into this world. I'd try to relive for her the events of the day, her tiny hands, the significant ways God answered our prayers, in startling detail. But other than those few nights when she would ask to hear her story, the details of that day—however monumental they were at the time—got lost in our memories. Day-to-day life eventually faded the once-vivid play-by-play. Nowadays I can go through extended periods of time without so much as a thought about that monumental day when I became a parent.

I wonder if that's how Mary and Joseph felt.

In a startlingly normal setting, could it be that, if Jesus had asked His parents to tell Him the story of His birth day, Joseph might have gotten a slightly nostalgic smile and said: "Ah . . . yes! That was quite a day. I forgot how cold that night was. We were so tired and sore from our journey to Bethlehem. Your mother and I couldn't believe it when she started the first contraction! Where were we going to stay? Ha! Thank goodness for that man who was kind enough to offer us that stable. (What was his name, Mary?) Your mother was such a champ. What a woman! And then all of a sudden, there you were—so, so tiny. Wow . . . Holding you for the first time is one of my all-time favorite memories, son. Oh, and that's right! There were these shepherds who came yelling into the cave, 'We've seen angels! Where is the baby king?' We've never known quite what to make of it, Jesus, but we have always known you are a special child. That was quite a night, son. All right, it's time for you to sleep now. Good-night, J."

And, perhaps, other than those nights when Jesus would ask to hear the stories, the small glimmers of divine that shone forth from His young life were lost in the mundane—in the ordinary. From the time they returned from Egypt until Jesus' first miracle at Cana (a span of perhaps twenty-five or twenty-six years), we know only that Jesus grew up. We read, "Jesus increased in wisdom and stature, and in favor with God and with people" (Luke 2:52). And in a prophecy from Isaiah, "He grew up before Him like a young plant and like a root out of dry ground. He didn't have an impressive majesty that we should look at Him, no appearance that we should desire Him" (Isa. 53:2–3).

Life in Joseph the carpenter's family was about as normal as normal gets, and (in case you've forgotten) normalcy rarely raises suspicion. Life was so normal, by and large, that they barely suspected the truth of their own son's identity! How else can you explain such tepid responses to all they saw and heard on Jesus' birth day, at His dedication, or when they found Jesus awing teachers in the temple at twelve years old? When the shepherds explained what the angels said about her new baby, "Mary was treasuring up all these things in her heart and meditating on them" (Luke 2:19). When, eight days later, Simeon came into the temple and boldly blessed their baby, calling Him God's salvation, Mary and Joseph were shocked by his words (Luke 2:33). When, twelve years later, they found Jesus in the temple, awing learned men with His wisdom, "they were astonished" (Luke 2:48). "They did not understand" why Jesus would say He belonged in His Father's house, so they mildly reprimanded Him and went home (Luke 2:50). Amazingly, what are we told again? "His mother kept all these things in her heart" (Luke 2:51).

I would have expected a little more confidence in her son's messiahship, even in those early years. Yet, at the same time, she was only human. And, to be fair, most of the "showier" signs were given to others, not to her. (She would not have seen the chorus of angels that appeared to the shepherds the night of Jesus' birth or perhaps even the bright star that guided the troop of magi.) Regardless of what she saw or didn't see, one thing seems obvious: The signs and wonders Mary saw in the first thirty years of Jesus' life were just vague enough to keep her guessing. The miraculous must not have been overt enough to overshadow the day-to-day realities of mothering an infant, toddler, or teenager. The space between the heavenly signs was filled with just the sort of ordinary occurrences that might have even made Mary and Joseph question whether they had imagined or exaggerated the significance of the signs altogether.

Have you ever wondered what might have filled the space between the apostles' narratives? What transpired between Jesus' birth and His first miracle at Cana? Apparently nothing worth the Gospel writers' ink. We are left to assume the details of His early life based on the details of our own, normal lives. Jesus got taller. His voice deepened. He probably learned to work at his father's business. He became a man, a wise man who found favor with the people who knew Him, and favor with God. But to most He was just Yeshua, Mary and Joseph's oldest kid—a small-town boy with a love for God. With such a common name, He could have been any Yosef, Loukas, or Yohanan! Nothing to raise the suspicion of his fellow Jews that He might be the long-awaited Christ, hidden in plain sight.

It was all just the way God wanted it.

Have you ever stopped to marvel that 90 percent of Jesus Christ's earthly life could be described much like ours? He spent roughly thirty of His thirty-three years living a largely ordinary life: being submissive to sinful parents, maturing, living, working, building relationships, studying and teaching the Scriptures, loving people, and loving God. We'd be simpletons to believe that a God who so obviously orchestrated His Son's birth and public ministry down to the minutest detail would leave the bulk of His life to happenstance. No, Christ's obscurity was as purposefully planned—and equally glorifying to God—as His journey to fame and His fall from the public's favor.

The Disposition of Christ

So Jesus grew up, much like you and I did. Then there was Cana. Jesus' first miracle began a three-year journey that has been the focus of most of Christendom's attention, and for good reason. In the narratives describing those three years of Christ's life, we learn the most about Him—His passion, His purpose, and His disposition.

His disposition fascinates me most these days. While reading and rereading the Gospel accounts, new facets of His character glimmer from the stories like flecks of mica in a chunk of granite. Listening to the dialogue between my Lord and the Pharisees, Sadducees, and other "important" religious minds of the day, I am astounded by Jesus's complete lack of concern over His reputation. In fact, at times it seemed He was purposefully out to sabotage His newfound "Christian famous" status (as seen in John 6 for example). His sometimes witty, sarcastic, even blunt responses to the self-important—well, He sure wasn't out to win any elections. He didn't crave the attention of the crowds, either. Even though He was forced to spend most of His time surrounded by fans, judging by the number of times we're told that Jesus ducked out of the crowds, He didn't base His worth on the accolades. He often went into seclusion to escape the fame and focus on His Father and His mission. A hillside in Galilee, a boat on Lake Genessaret, the Mount of Olives just outside Jerusalem—all places to escape others' accolades, expectations, and demands and just *be*.

In case we've forgotten, God is *unabashedly* committed to His own glory (see Ps. 106:8; Isa. 42:8; 43:25; and Ezek. 36:22, for starters). Notice that whether obscure or thrust into the spotlight, *every* day of Christ's life was spent bringing glory to His Father. While living in obscurity, Jesus brought the Father glory by loving and serving God and others. And in His so-called heyday, Jesus brought the Father glory by loving and serving God and others.

Words that describe the disposition of the Christ we see in Scripture: *humble, thankful, righteous, a servant*—His only ambition to submit to His Father's will. He was consumed with loving God and those around Him.

Words that describe many of Christ's followers (Christian famous or otherwise): *proud, greedy, sinful, self-focused*—our most driving ambition to free ourselves from having to rely on the Father (i.e., self-sufficiency). We are consumed with ourselves and use those around us for our own advancement.

Christ brought the Father glory by becoming nothing (Phil. 2:5-11). If He is our example in everything, it follows that we also will glorify our God when we embrace an

This must be an all-encompassing ATTITUDE

obscurity of heart for His sake and for the sake of others. We are told, "Make your own attitude that of Christ Jesus" (Phil. 2:5). Yet interestingly enough, our current M.O. appears alarmingly similar to another disposition of which we learn in Scripture: Lucifer's.

Opposing Dispositions

Read Philippians 2:6–8 with me again.

[Christ Jesus], existing in the form of God, did not consider equality with God as something to be used for His own advantage. Instead He emptied Himself by assuming the form of a slave, taking on the likeness of men. And when He had come as a man in His external form, He humbled Himself by becoming obedient to the point of death—even to death on a cross.

Now consider what follows, in verses 9–11.

For this reason God also highly exalted Him and gave Him the name that is above every name, so that at the name of Jesus every knee should bow—of those who are in heaven and on earth and under the earth—and every tongue should confess that Jesus Christ is Lord, to the glory of God the Father.

Christ's life epitomizes Proverbs 15:33: "*Humility* comes before *honor*" (NIV, emphasis added). Not primarily honor in His brief earthly life but in life after death for eternity hereafter. Now that may sound simple at first glance, but in practice, wouldn't our flesh like to switch out a word there? Maybe *recognition* followed by honor, *appreciation* followed by honor, or *fame* followed by honor? Don't those seem more natural? But at the root of our desire to change the substance of that first sentence, we find the disposition of one diametrically opposed to our humble King: Satan.

Consider these passages, which describe Lucifer's disposition:

> Shining morning star, how you have fallen from the heavens! You destroyer of nations, you have been cut down to the ground. You said to yourself: "I will ascend to the heavens; I will set up my throne above the stars of God. I will sit on the mount of the gods' assembly, in the remotest parts of the North. I will ascend above the highest clouds; I will make myself like the Most High." But you will be brought down to Sheol into the deepest regions of the Pit. Those who see you will stare at you; they will look closely at you: "Is this the man who caused the earth to tremble, who shook the kingdoms?" (Isa. 14:12–16)

> This is what the Lord GOD says: You were the seal of perfection, full of wisdom and perfect in beauty. You were in Eden, the garden of God. Every kind of precious stone covered you. . . . Your mountings and settings were crafted in gold; they were prepared on the day you were created. You were an anointed guardian cherub, for I had appointed you. You were on the holy mountain of God; you walked among the fiery stones. From the day you were created you were blameless in your ways until wickedness was found in you. Through the abundance of your trade, you were filled with violence, and you sinned. So I expelled you

in disgrace from the mountain of God, and banished you, guardian cherub, from among the fiery stones. Your heart became proud because of your beauty; for the sake of your splendor you corrupted your wisdom. So I threw you down to the earth I made you a spectacle before kings. (Ezek. 28:12–17)

Satan's life is one of *pride* followed by *humiliation* (the worst of which is yet to come).

Christ's Disposition (Phil. 2:5–11)	Satan's Disposition (Isa. 14:12–16; Ezek. 28:12–17)
Is by His very nature God (v. 6)	Is by nature created by God (Ezek. 28:15)
Did not cling to His rights of deity, even though they belonged to Him (v. 6)	Pursued the rights of deity, even though they did not belong to him (Isa. 14:13–14)
Humbled Himself; made Himself of *no* reputation (v. 7)	Bragged incessantly in his heart (Isa. 14:13–14)
Came to serve men, His created ones (v. 7)	Sought to rule over those he did not create (Isa. 14:13–14)
God Angels } Became Man	God Angels } Tried to Become Man
Chose obedience to the will of God, even though it included obscurity and even death (v. 8)	Rebelled against the will of God because even the beauty, wisdom, high position, and privileges given him weren't enough (Isa. 14:13–14; Exek. 28:12–15)

Therefore . . .	Therefore . . .
God has exalted Him (v. 9)	God has cast him down (Isa. 14:12; Ezek. 28:17)
Every knee will bow to Him, in heaven and on earth (v. 10)	Heaven and earth will marvel at his destruction (Isa. 14:16)
God is glorified (v. 11)	God is glorified
Life Summarized	**Life Summarized**
Humility followed by *honor*	*Pride* followed by *humiliation*

Do you resonate with the differences between Christ's disposition and Satan's? How unnerving to consider that, left to ourselves, we continually pamper the same pride that led Lucifer down the path of perdition. Consider with me . . .

- Do you ever pursue the rights of deity (power, omniscience, the right to judge people's thoughts and intentions), even though they do not belong to you?
- Are you boastful—verbally or in the privacy of your heart?
- Do you seek to rule over those you have not created— perhaps not in a governmental sense but emotionally or spiritually?
- Do you ever rebel against God's will for your life (i.e., choose your way over His) because even the (relatively) high position you've been given isn't enough for you?

Unless we stop imitating our enemy, we can be absolutely certain that we will also reap the same end: ultimate (perhaps even eternal) humiliation. Maybe it's time for us to wake up and embrace a different disposition.

Embracing the Humble King

In a ludicrous act of humility and grace, Christ came. The Supreme Being of the universe came to Earth as a helpless baby, was raised within the confines of obscurity, and—at the height of His brief "success"—the crowds turned on Him and unfairly nailed Him to a cross like a common criminal. The Alpha and Omega was purposefully confined to time and space, just like you and me. He had to wait in line at the market right next to His neighbors, and He got dust in His sandals when He walked. He likely felt the demands of His job, disappointed others, and felt the sting of rejection. He lost people He loved, had to deal with people who hated His guts, and was misunderstood and misquoted.

He did all of this out of love for us and for His glory, the two of which—you'll remember—are beautifully and eternally juxtaposed.

Have you marveled lately at Christ's selfless humility? I readily admit that I, for one, have been too busy pursuing my own ambitions—best-sellers' lists, dreams of a home by the sea, and for heaven's sake, rock-hard abs—to really and truly *marvel,* let alone allow His disposition to overtake mine.

But now that you and I *have* (hopefully) marveled, no more ludicrathetic living! Let's daily awe at God's unlikely rescue plan. Let's allow the profound simplicity of Christ's godly ambitions to overshadow our worldly dreams and desires. Let's daily *incinerate* our pride on the altar. As we learn to embrace our humble King, we might just come to appreciate our true and right place in this world: We are nothing. *He* is everything.

Discussion Questions

1. If you were a god, and you were designing a messiah to come and save humanity, what would your own "divine cocktail of history's best" look like?

2. Since God was capable of building the finest Messiah-Machine imaginable, the earthly circumstances of our Lord, Jesus Christ, should be cause for reflection. What two or three things strike you most about Jesus' birth, life, and death?

3. Jesus—*God's own Son*—spent roughly 90 percent of His earthly life in strikingly normal circumstances. How does Jesus' largely ordinary life affect the way you view your own life?

4. Jesus spent roughly three years in visible ministry. How would you describe His disposition during that time? What do we learn about His character through the gospel narratives?

5. In stark contrast to Christ's selfless humility, there's Satan and his desire to be greatest. In honest reflection, whose disposition do you most closely mirror?

6. What do we need to do in order to stop imitating our enemy?

7. Can you think of any practical ways we can win the battle over our own "ludicratheticity" and more often marvel at God's incredible act of mercy: *the Gospel*?

8. How might you need to let the profound simplicity of Christ's godly ambitions overshadow your worldly dreams and desires?

CHAPTER 4

Embracing Significance

Remember, dear brothers and sisters, that few of you were wise in the world's eyes or powerful or wealthy when God called you. Instead, God chose things the world considers foolish in order to shame those who think they are wise. And he chose things that are powerless to shame those who are powerful. God chose things despised by the world, things counted as nothing at all, and used them to bring to nothing what the world considers important. As a result, no one can ever boast in the presence of God.

1 Corinthians 1:26–29 (NLT)

It was no great compliment when God called you to follow Jesus Christ.

Nope, not for me either. "Foolish," "powerless," "despised," and "nothing at all" are hardly complimentary.

It might seem strange to start a chapter on significance with yet another reminder that we are among the common things of this world, but, as I think you'll come to see, that's exactly when our true significance takes the stage. After Paul gets done insulting the Corinthian believers in verses 26–29, his next words are revolutionary:

God has united you with Christ Jesus. (v. 30 NLT)

In other words, you might be dumb, weak, shunned, and obscure; but if you love and follow Jesus, Paul says, then you've been joined to true significance. You've got "it," not based on your works but on Christ's. You don't have to waste your life earning momentary kudos from the world. Instead, eternal significance is yours in an instant through embracing the work of Christ. Paul goes on to say:

For our benefit God made him to be wisdom itself. Christ made us right with God; he made us pure and holy, and he freed us from sin. Therefore, as the Scriptures say, "If you want to boast, boast only about the Lord." (1 Cor. 1:30–31 NLT)

Now there's a reason to boast!

We've talked quite a bit about our misguided search for significance—our quest for success, wealth, notoriety, power, or to be in some way, *any* way, different. What we haven't asked so far is *why?* Why do we crave to be "somebody"? Why do seven billion planet-mates make us feel small? Why are we on the hunt to find meaning and purpose in our achievements, recognition, occupations, and relationships?

Perhaps these are questions we can't completely answer this side of eternity. We do know, however, that when God created the first man and the first woman, He equipped them with a design feature that essentially preprogrammed every human thereafter to crave Him, desire Him. It would ensure that no matter how far Adam and Eve strayed from Him, they would only feel complete once they returned. And perhaps our desire to be significant is part of this divine homing device. Could it be that God embedded in each of us a desire to be significant, knowing it would be one of the things to draw His elect to Him? Because the truth is, if we really want to feel worth (in the deepest, truest sense of the word), we need look no further than the cross. In Calvary we find that we are the treasure in the greatest pursuit of all time.

Let's recap:

- Supreme Being of the universe creates man.
- Man rejects God.
- God becomes man and rescues you and me by living and dying sinlessly. Those who repent and trust Christ are joined to our significant Savior (receiving all benefits).

Don't let the simplicity of the love story numb you to the implications of this unlikely romance. *We are the object of His desire.* We, who are dust, and He, who is everything and needs nothing.

Like many of our preprogrammed homing devices (a desire to be loved, to create, to nurture, etc.), we usually search in all the wrong places before we find our hearts' true longing. But if we'd get over ourselves long enough to embrace where our true significance lies—and how radical it truly is!—we'd search no further than the installer Himself.

Exponential Significance

Did you ever play with those magic bath capsules as a kid? You know, those colorful little pill-looking shapes that you drop in the tub and then wait . . . wait . . . wait—POP! Out comes a tiny green camel or a purple foam penguin. Who knew how much fun you could have with some colored foam and a clear casing, right? Those things are awesome. All that potential hiding out in plain sight, just waiting to explode at the first touch of bathwater.

Our significance is like that. All people, whether or not they choose to give their lives to God, have value because they were created by God (Rev. 4:11) and have been made in His own image (Gen. 1:26–27). We have significance because we exist in the plan of the only omni-God. Even the likes of Pharaoh, King Herod, and King Ahab—all known for their dastardly deeds—were significant precisely because God raised them up to play villain in His story of the ages, thus bringing glory to Himself (see Rom. 9:17–18; Col. 1:16).

Before redemption, each man, woman, and child is a lot like one of those magic bath capsules: each has value but also has the potential to be so much more. But get this: Once we embrace Jesus Christ as Lord, we are transformed by the first touch of living water, and our significance *explodes*! We become what we were always intended to be: *right with God*. Are you getting this? The facets of our significance in Christ—our redemption itself, the work of the Spirit, the fervor of our suitor, the assurance of our inheritance, and the purpose in our calling—are like a whole *herd* of animals stuffed into one magic bath capsule! When we surrender and embrace Christ, all the potential that was once crammed inside becomes kinetic.

It's a quirky analogy, I know. Maybe Romans 3:23–25 says it better:

> For all have sinned and fall short of the glory of God. They are justified freely by His grace through the redemption that is in Christ Jesus. God presented Him as a propitiation through faith in His blood, to demonstrate His righteousness, because in His restraint God passed over the sins previously committed.

The moment we are "justified freely" by accepting Christ's gift of salvation—when we stop running from God and simply embrace His undeserved kindness toward us—we find significance. We find our heart's longing. In a moment Christ's life, death, and resurrection are ours by faith.

The world is in a frenzy trying to find lasting, eternal significance. But their efforts are in vain. Only God has ultimate, eternal significance, and the only way we mortals get it is by joining our lives to His. Instead of spending our days struggling for significance, living under the shame of failure, and watching what temporary significance we do achieve fade away, Christ offers His significant life to us all. We cannot earn it; we simply receive it by faith. He *is* our significance.

Going back to the bath, the first aspect of our significance in Christ, then, is that we are no longer confined to potential. We're no longer in capsule form, if you will. Christ's righteousness is assigned to us (such grace!) when we believe. We acquire all the worth that comes from being completely righteous through our substitute, and—POP! We've been baptized into living water; we've been freed from the cage of sin and have taken a more significant form: new life in Christ. But, as promised, there's more. Much more.

Significance in the Spirit

Another element of our significance as believers is the Holy Spirit whom God has sent to fill our hearts as a guarantee until we reach heaven. He didn't give us His Spirit because we were significant, but rather, we are significant because *He* is *uber*-significant, and *He* is within us! This powerful Spirit allows us to:

- Come to the Father for salvation (Eph. 2:18; 2 Thess. 2:13).
- Be led into truth (John 14:17, 26; 1 John 2:27).
- Know the deep secrets of God and understand the things He has given us (1 Cor. 2:10, 12).
- Be filled with God's love and know God's love for us (Rom. 5:5).
- Be freed from the power of sin in our lives (Rom. 8:2).
- Have power from heaven for God's purposes (Luke 24:49; Acts 1:8).
- Speak truth (Matt. 10:20).
- Be confident that we are God's children and assured of what He has promised us as such (Rom. 8:14–16; 2 Cor. 1:22; Eph. 1:13–14).
- Have help in our weakness (Rom. 8:26).
- Receive spiritual gifts (1 Cor. 12:4).
- Produce spiritual fruit like love, joy, peace, patience, kindness, goodness, faithfulness, gentleness, and self-control (Gal. 5:22–23).
- Renew our thoughts and attitudes (Eph. 4:23).
- Be united as believers (Eph. 4:3).
- Love others (Col. 1:8).

- Have a spirit of love, power, and self-discipline (2 Tim. 1:7).
- Be raised from death as Christ was (Rom. 8:10–11; 1 Pet. 4:6).

The Holy Spirit gives us spiritual life and abides in us (John 3:6; 6:36; 14:16–18). He is the proof that God lives in us (1 John 4:13), and He prays endlessly on our behalf (Rom. 8:26–27). Got all that? Now . . .

We are called *His sanctuary* (1 Cor. 6:19).

How could the dwelling place of this living Spirit *not* be of value? Think of it this way: If the Holy Spirit chose to make the Managua City Dump His residence, every rotting rind and discarded diaper would instantly be worth more than all the gold in all the treasuries in all the world. Yet He *has* chosen to make His home within men, women, and children—even some who live in that dump—making their worth outshine the combined original value of every item they live among.[1] Likewise, we have that magnitude of worth, and more, simply because the Holy Spirit resides in us.

Significance in Our Union

As a bridegroom rejoices over [his] bride, so your God will rejoice over you. (Isa. 62:5)

For the husband is the head of the wife as also Christ is head of the church. He is the Savior of the body. . . . Christ loved the church and gave Himself for her to make her holy, cleansing her with the washing of water by the word. He did this to present the church to Himself in splendor, without spot or wrinkle or anything like that, but holy and blameless. . . . This mystery is profound, but I am talking about Christ and the church. (Eph. 5:25–27)

Normally I would caution against finding our significance in any relationship, especially in a marriage partner, or in the illusive "one" who we feel confirms our worth. But in this case it is completely appropriate (and necessary) for us to find our worth in another. This "spouse" can *and does* ensure our value, and we can take great pride in being called His. Better than any well-groomed Hollywood Casanova with polished rhetoric and swoon-worthy smile, consider this picture of your heavenly Groom:

And among the lampstands was One like the Son of Man, dressed in a long robe, and with a gold sash wrapped around His chest. His head and hair were white like wool—white as snow, His eyes like a fiery flame, His feet like fine bronze fired in a furnace, and His voice like the sound of cascading waters. In His right hand He had seven stars; from His mouth came a sharp two-edged sword; and His face was shining like the sun at midday. When I saw Him I fell at His feet like a dead man. He laid His right hand on me, and said, "Don't be afraid! I am the First and the Last, and the Living One. I was dead, but look—I am alive forever and ever, and I hold the keys of death and Hades. (Rev. 1:13–18)

Admittedly, some men have difficulty appreciating the analogy of Christ being the church's *husband*. But bear with me for a moment. If just the overwhelming sight of your "significant other" caused you to faint dead away, don't you think you'd have reason to boast? If your spouse spoke with the authority of crashing waves, had eyes that shone like flames, and walked around wielding a double-edged sword *from His mouth,* we'd all excuse you for thinking you were "someone." You *would be* someone, just for being His.

Christ calls us His *bride.* I'm afraid this has become yet another "ludicrathetic" fact to us, His loved ones. *Savor* these truths: He desires you, pursues you, purifies and delights in you! He moved heaven and earth so He could be near you. He's gone to get the house ready, and waits anxiously for your arrival.

Would a perfect, almighty Groom go through all that trouble for trash? Again, we see that our worth is implied by the great love with which He loves us—this time, as our marriage partner.

Significance in Our Inheritance

A good friend of mine was adopted as an infant. A loving, God-fearing couple took him in and called him their own. They named him, changed his diapers, paid for his braces, sent him to college, and gave him all the love they could. Even in some hard teenage years, they never rescinded their commitment to be dad and mom. And because he is their true son through adoption, he is also named in their will as an heir. He and I have talked about the sheer grace involved in his situation. He, who had absolutely no right to *anything* of theirs, shares in *everything* they are and own.

Now here's the wild part. God has adopted *you.* He has named you, comforted you, disciplined and provided for you. And because you are His true son or daughter, He has also named you in His "will" to be an equal heir with your divine brother, Jesus Christ. Can you wrap your mind around the sheer grace involved in *your* situation? You, who have absolutely no right to *anything* of God's, share in *everything* He is and owns.

> You received God's Spirit when he adopted you as his own children. Now we call him, "Abba, Father." For his Spirit joins with our spirit to affirm that we are God's children. And since we are his children, we are his heirs. In fact, together with Christ we are heirs of God's glory. (Rom. 8:15–17 NLT)

The scenario has significance written all over it. Again, not because of anything we've done or could do to earn it but because of God's unending grace. If a man or woman has greater significance because of the adoption and inheritance of earthly parents, how much more do we have because of our divine adoptive Father?

Here's a little taste of the *significant* inheritance we have to look forward to:

Taste 1: Being raised from the dead and sharing in Christ's glory.

> But now Christ has been raised from the dead, the first-fruits of those who have fallen asleep. For since death came through a man, the resurrection of the dead also comes through a man. For just as in Adam all die, so also in Christ all will be made alive. But each in his own order: Christ, the firstfruits; afterward, at His coming, those who belong to Christ. (1 Cor. 15:20–23)

> For you have died, and your life is hidden with the Messiah in God. When the Messiah, who is your life, is revealed, then you also will be revealed with Him in glory. (Col. 3:3–4)

Taste 2: An awesome new body. Can I get an *amen?*

> And we believers also groan, even though we have the Holy Spirit within us as a foretaste of future glory, for we long for our bodies to be released from sin and suffering. We, too, wait with eager hope for the day when God will give us our full rights as his adopted children, including the new bodies he has promised us. (Rom. 8:23 NLT)

> The sun has one kind of glory, while the moon and stars each have another kind. And even the stars differ from each other in their glory. It is the same way with the resurrection of the dead. Our earthly bodies are planted in the ground when we die, but they will be raised to live forever. Our bodies are buried in brokenness, but they will be raised in glory. They are buried in weakness, but they will be raised in strength. (1 Cor. 15:41–43 NLT)

Taste 3: An eternal home where we will never have to be far from our Lord Jesus again.

> Your heart must not be troubled. Believe in God; believe also in Me. In My Father's house are many dwelling places; if not, I would have told you. I am going away to prepare a place for you. If I go away and prepare a place for you, I will come back and receive you to Myself, so that where I am you may be also. (John 14:1–3)

Just as my friend is experiencing some of his "rights" of adoption while his parents are alive (their love, discipline, wisdom, care, and generous birthday presents), his "full rights" as an adopted child will only be realized after their death. The same is true for us. While we experience God's love, discipline, wisdom, care, and generous provisions in this life, we have to wait for death (in this case, ours) before we will know and take hold of the bulk of our inheritance as God's children.

Ephesians 1:14 says that God has promised this inheritance "so we would praise and glorify him" (NLT). Would you take a moment to do that now?

SIGNIFICANCE IN OUR ROLE

When we accept that our value is not dependent on what we do or accomplish, we are ironically liberated to do much for Christ. Not "much" in the ways for which we've striven up to this point, but "much" in terms of fulfilling the two greatest commandments: loving God and loving others (Matt. 22:34–40). It makes sense, doesn't it? How can we possibly love God or love others from a pure heart while we're chasing after frivolities to confirm our value?

I've long suspected that one of Satan's most effective tactics in immobilizing modern believers is a simple mirror. Not a physical mirror but a mental and spiritual one. Like Narcissus, we have become so self-absorbed that we can't see past ourselves. What good can we do for God's kingdom when we spend most of our lives in front of a mirror, introspectively picking at our "pimples" instead of living a life of purpose and power?

That's the beauty of finding our significance in Christ: we are freed from our vanity and can instead fulfill God's purposes for us. What are those purposes? Perhaps that's a book for another day, but here are a few to whet your appetite. Embracing your true significance frees you to:

- Love God with your whole heart, soul, and strength (Deut. 6:5; Luke 10:27).
- Become increasingly like Christ, imitating God and living a life of love (1 Cor. 11:1; Eph. 5:1–2).
- Be a conduit of His love to others (1 Cor. 13).
- Be salt and light to the world (Matt. 5:13–16).
- Serve others in the name of Christ (Matt. 10:41–42; Phil. 2:3–4).
- Fight God's enemies as a true spiritual contender (Eph. 6:10–18; 2 Cor. 10:3–4).

God gave Adam and Eve "jobs" before they sinned. Something to "do" was part of God's perfect plan for them and for us. We are designed to find pleasure and purpose in the roles God has given us—relationally, vocationally, and spiritually. In another word, we find *significance* in playing a part in God's great screenplay of the ages. And when we find our significance in Christ, we can be content to play a supporting role or even to stand in as an "extra" in the background. The visibility of our part stops being such a big deal, as the reality of being on the cast *at all* sinks in.

Redefining *Valuable*

Our truest and greatest significance in life comes from our inherent value in Christ. I realize that sounds redundant—having *significance* because of our *value*—but only because we're confused about the spiritual meaning of "valuable." We tend to view our value in Christ as a *Webster's* definition kind of valuable:

valuable (adj.)—1. a: having monetary value; b: worth a good price; 2. a: having desirable or esteemed characteristics or qualities; b: of great use or service[2]

This definition works well to describe employees, islands and diamonds, but spiritually speaking it will never do. From God's point of view, our value isn't derived from how much money we're worth, our great qualities or even our useful service. Our true and eternal value comes from something completely outside ourselves.

As I write this, a dizzying whirlwind of snow falls onto already white trees, houses, and streets. Millions of flakes swirl and dance in their free-fall from the clouds. Trying to follow just one flake from the grey sky above to the white blanket of ground is an exercise in futility. There are just too many of them, and they fall too quickly. Here's a thought: *How many* gazillions *of snowflakes have fallen throughout history?* It has snowed in every continent in every year of every generation of every millennium. How many individual flakes have formed and fallen from the sky in that time? Some small, dense, and dry; others as light and fluffy as goose down. Some falling unseen, others the focus of rapt attention, the answer to the heartfelt prayers of a child for a white Christmas. Let's get to the point—there are a bunch! Does each of those innumerable flakes of snow have significance? Do they matter? The answer is yes, for two reasons.

A single flake of snow won't do much to water Earth, but it is part of a much grander, understatedly vital irrigation system. For that reason alone it is important. But the other source of significance has nothing to do with the flake itself. In fact, the snowflake couldn't have done anything to contribute to its value. We know that each of the gazillions of snowflakes is significant because a Master Designer took time to make each one absolutely unique. "Experts" (whoever "they" are) say that no two snowflakes have ever been exactly the same. *Ever.* Incredible, isn't it? The fact that God took pains to give each one a unique crystal structure all its own gives that snowflake intrinsic value. Again, there is nothing any snowflake can do to add or detract from that value. It comes from a source completely outside itself. Likewise, we are valuable because of the intrinsic worth that comes from being designed by, enjoyed by, and given purpose by the Creator.

There's a difference between feeling significant or desired because you are needed or because someone wants you to do something *for* them (to fill up their lacking), and being significant and desired by someone simply because He *delights* in you. *You*—not what you can do *for* Him. This is significance without strings: Value that's not contingent on what you do or accomplish but entirely dependent on what He has done in creating you, redeeming you, calling you, and leading you.

God calls you by name. In fact, He knows everything about you, watches your every move, cares to know every inconsequential thought you have throughout the day. He knows you so well, He can tell you what you're going to say, even before you say it. When you need someone to lead you, He's on up ahead. When you need someone to get your back, He's right behind you. No matter how far you wander, He's right beside you. He can't get enough of blessing you, guiding you, letting His light shine on you. If God were a scrapbooker, He'd have books and books of every memory of your life— from the moment you were conceived till the day you die— and beyond. And He thinks about you more often than you could ever count. (Paraphrase of John 10:1–16 and Ps. 139.)

Is *that* significant enough for you?

This extraordinary knowledge is beyond me. It is lofty; I am unable to reach it. (Ps. 139:6)

I hope so. Because we can't embrace obscurity until we reject the world's shallow views of significance and instead find our true and lasting worth in Christ. Only this kind of significance produces the confidence we'll need to live our lives following in the footsteps of our humble King.

Discussion Questions

1. First Corinthians 1:31 teaches that if we're going to boast, we must "boast only about the LORD" (NLT). In a world dead-set on promoting self, what kind of reactions from others do you think you would get if you obeyed this command?

2. Why do you think we have such a desire to be "somebody"? Do you think that drive is based solely on our pride, or what other factors might be at play?

3. Why do you think we're on the hunt to find meaning and purpose in our achievements, recognition, occupations, and relationships?

4. Briefly explain five sources of our significance in Christ:
    1.
    2.
    3.
    4.
    5.

5. Which of those five sources of significance means the most to you personally?

6. How does God define your "value"?

7. We spend most of our lives trying to prove how valuable we are—to our friends, our coworkers and families, and even to our God. How might God's offer of "significance without strings" revolutionize your life?

8. How does a right understanding of your own significance, through Christ, enable you to embrace obscurity *gladly*?

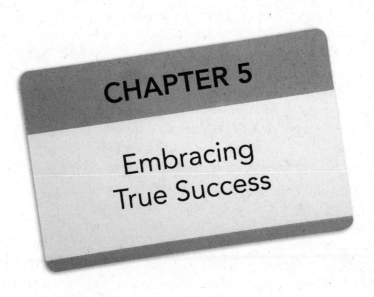

CHAPTER 5

Embracing True Success

*The world offers only a craving for physical pleasure,
a craving for everything we see, and pride in our
achievements and possessions. These are not from the
Father, but are from this world.*

1 JOHN 2:16 (NLT)

*Why do we take consolation from celebrity Christians
who judge success by the standards of the world?
Why do we take our cues from people so conspicuously
different than Jesus? Why do we listen to men who,
had they lived in the first century, would have sold
tickets to the feeding of the five thousand and charged
a fee to watch the raising of Lazarus?*

RANDY ALCORN[1]

Tom had a ten thousand-acre ranch near Jackson Hole, Wyoming. The land was some of the best in the area, and home to roughly eleven thousand cattle and horses. His house? A custom log home along the Snake River. He employed twenty-five ranch hands, groundskeepers, housekeepers, and a nanny for the youngest of his ten children. You might think the success of his ranch would have given him a cocky, John Wayne swagger to his step, but you'd be hard pressed to find a nicer guy. Tom loved God and loved his family. He was so worried about his kids' salvation that he'd pray for them daily—sometimes for an hour or more.

From the world's point of view, Tom had it all. But what did God think of his success? Was He impressed? Did He frown on Tom's fortune? Neither actually. But He did take it all away, in one fell swoop. Nothing left. House gone. Animals gone. Family gone. All that was left was Tom, and from God's point of view, he was just as successful as ever. You see, Tom (aka, Job), wasn't successful in God's eyes because of his wealth, greatness, or even his large family. God said, "No one else on the earth is like him," because "[he is] a man of perfect integrity, who fears God and turns away from evil" (Job 1:8).

Job's story gives us a glimpse into God's take on success—what it is, what it isn't, and how we should view it when we have it. First John 2:15–17 gives us further, critical advice:

> Do not love this world nor the things it offers you, for when you love the world, you do not have the love of the Father in you. For the world offers only a craving for physical pleasure, a craving for everything we see, and pride in our achievements and possessions. These are not from the Father, but are from this world. And this world is fading away, along with everything that

people crave. But anyone who does what pleases God will live forever. (NLT)

You've likely heard this passage before; you might even have it memorized. So to combat the familiarity, let's take it apart and see if we can't squeeze some fresh insight out of it.

Behind door number one, we have what the world offers. Loving (not necessarily *having*, but loving) any of these four vices eventually destroys us from the inside out: (1) craving physical pleasure, (2) craving more and more stuff, (3) taking pride in our achievements, and (4) taking pride in our stuff. Cravings and pride. While the latter category speaks more directly to our discussion of embracing obscurity, the two usually go together like coffee and creamer.

If you've ever heard a sermon on 1 John 2:15–17, then you've likely also heard that physical pleasure, material things, and achievements aren't of themselves *wrong*. But let's not fool ourselves. We're human. We stink at avoiding excess and pride, both of which *are* sins. Couple human (i.e., sin) nature with the cultural bullhorn in the background, encouraging us to go for our dreams and take the cake as a snack for later, and we're in dangerous territory. Dreaming big is an easy sell! You don't have to do much convincing to make us believe that we are capable of "making it," and—here's the crux—we *deserve* to. Peel back the layers of innocent ambition and desires for provision in each of us, and you'll find hiding in the shadows a greedy fiend that makes our culture's feel-good mantra especially appealing and *dangerous*.

I don't think we realize how far we've come in imitating the world's tenets of success or just how *dangerous* that is. I'm shocked at how easily my friends, family, church, and I have swallowed the lie—hook, line, and sinker—that true fulfillment will greet them on the other side of a PhD and a six-figure income, through a romantic comedy-esque love story, or even through leading a prominent ministry. I'm alarmed at how pride and self-promotion are permeating Christian leadership and how it seems to be seeping down the ranks: to you, to me, to our kids, and throughout our congregations. If you understand the cancerous nature of pride, you can fathom just how scary our situation has become.

So how do we recognize which faulty views of success we have adopted from the world and which are truly of God? Let's take a closer look at 1 John 2:15–17 and try to distinguish our cravings and pride from God's true measures of success.

Craving for Physical Pleasure

What does an overworking craving for physical pleasure look like? It's easy to point the finger at "them," those blatant hedonists of the world (like greedy dictators with lavish castles and starving subjects), but what if this sin resides a bit closer to home? How might you and I falter in this area? Just a few ideas to get us thinking:

- **Food.** Rather, our overindulgence of it. I think it's fair to say that we eat food primarily for pleasure rather than primarily for fuel, and our waistlines are the judge and jury. The percentage of us who are overweight or obese is startling, yet there is no shortage of patrons at every taste-bud-tantalizing establishment across the country, even in economic hard times.
- **Sex (outside of marriage).** How many crave the rush of pleasurable hormones that come from "friends with benefits," pornography, and sexual addiction?

Apparently a whole lot. Thirty-five percent of "born-again Christians" think having a sexual relationship with someone of the opposite sex to whom they are not married is "morally acceptable." About half think it's fine to have sexual thoughts or fantasies about someone else.[2] These are just two examples in a long line of horrifying statistics. No wonder more Christians are enslaved to sexual immorality than ever before.

- **Comfort.** Ever heard of a dream home in the Arctic or a resort marketed as "adequately comfortable"? I think not. We don't want to be too hot, too cold, too thirsty, too dry, or too dirty, and we're willing to rearrange substantial parts of our lives to avoid discomfort of any kind (mental, physical, or spiritual).

- **Mood-Altering Substances.** How many multimillion-dollar industries feed off our desire to chase the blues away? We've got Starbucks, Marlborough, Budweiser, Coke, Red Bull, Red Man, and Redline Rush. And if the natural high of adrenaline is more to your taste, then there's skydiving, bungee jumping, white-water rafting, paragliding, swimming with sharks, and hanging by a thread over a five-hundred-foot cave. Apparently we no longer have any excuse not to feel good.

- **Various and Sundry Feel-Good Items.** We're willing to pay—sometimes big bucks—for all sorts of things that give us that feel-good bliss. Massage chairs, hot tubs, feather beds, automobile seat heaters, saunas, and silk sheets, just to name a few.

I'll say it again: feeling good isn't evil. God gave us our senses for a reason. But our *over*-desire for pleasure chases even a sincere love for God right out of our hearts. Jesus said it best, "Where your treasure is, there your heart will be also" (Matt. 6:21). Speaking of treasure . . .

Craving for Material Things

Some have called our condition *affluenza*: "a painful, contagious, socially transmitted condition of overload, debt, anxiety and waste resulting from the dogged pursuit of more."[3] The Bible has a simpler term for our illness: greed. And because our greed can seem so harmless, so innocent, so *justified*, Jesus sternly warned us to be always on guard against it: "Beware! Guard against every kind of greed. Life is not measured by how much you own" (Luke 12:15 NLT). Then, as was often His custom, He told a story that hits frighteningly close to home. It went something like this:

> There was once a man who had a job that paid him more than he truly needed. The man said to himself, "What should I do? I've already bought a house and filled it with nice furnishings. I have plenty of food, a closet full of clothes, two cars, and a boat." Then he said, "I know! I'll fill up my 401k and IRA accounts to ensure that I'll be able to live like this for years to come. Then I'll be able to sit back and say to myself, 'By jove, good man, you're set for life. Now you can relax, play as much golf as you'd like, and take your wife to the Riviera.'" But God said, "You idiot! You're going to die tonight, and then who will get everything you've worked so hard for?" (Luke 12:16–20, author's paraphrase)

When He finished the story, He could likely tell that everyone listening was thinking of *those* rich people (rather than searching their own hearts), so He finished with yet another warning, just to make sure they (and we) *really* got it: "That's how it is with the one who stores up treasure for himself and is not rich toward God" (Luke 12:21). But even in reading that word "treasure," we have a tendency to ignore the root of our own personal version of greed. Plasma TVs, iPhones, and hobby equipment seem more of a necessity nowadays than a luxury, and so we miss Jesus' point. A. W. Tozer exposes the seriousness of our deception:

> There is within the human heart a tough, fibrous root of fallen life whose nature is to possess, always to possess. It covets things with a deep and fierce passion. The pronouns *my* and *mine* look innocent enough in print, but their constant and universal use is significant. They express the real nature of the old Adamic man better than a thousand volumes of theology could do. They are verbal symptoms of our deep disease. The roots of our hearts have grown down into things, and we dare not pull up one rootlet lest we die. Things have become necessary to us, a development never originally intended. God's gifts now take the place of God, and the whole course of nature is upset by the monstrous substitution.[4]

Affluenza infects many Christians as potently as it does the rest of mankind. This should not be! How can the Holy Spirit work in and through us when we've buried Him chest-deep in the trinkets and souvenirs we've collected in this life? Asceticism isn't the answer (Jesus was certainly no ascetic). No, the antibiotic for affluenza is a serum of one part simplicity, one part humility, and one hundred parts Christlikeness. Christ is our pattern in all things, including our view of earthly paraphernalia.

Pride in Our Achievements

We've already mentioned many of the achievements we run after, so I'm not going to relist them all here. You know what accomplishments you have been most proud of in the past, are most proud of now, and those for which your heart can't stop pining. Is it a degree? An album? How about a big family to fill your big house? Do you live in the past glory of winning a big game? Do you make sure others hear about your recent promotion or award-winning marriage proposal? Have you ever left a little bit of acrylic smudged on your arm after completing a painting? Are you dreaming of making it onto the cover of *Working Mom Magazine*?

You've done some cool things. Good for you . . . truly. Just don't let them define you. To echo chapter 2, don't let them become your subtitle. Taking pride in what we accomplish—including all the subtle little successes the world advertises—leaves little room for humility. How can a love for the Father thrive when it's being choked out by ambition? Reminds me of another parable Jesus taught:

> The sower sows the word . . . [Some seeds] are sown among thorns; these are the ones who hear the word, but the *worries of this age,* the *seduction of wealth,* and the *desires for other things* enter in and choke the word, and it becomes unfruitful. (Mark 4:14, 18–19, emphasis added)

Pride in Our Possessions

Perhaps the only difference between craving a particular possession and taking pride in it is the simple act of acquisition. If I desire something so badly that I'm ready to sacrifice important things to get it, pride in that item is sure to follow. The only way to avoid taking pride in what we have, then, is to have a healthy, God-centered, stewardship-minded view of all material stuff in the first place. It's pretty simple, really. How can I take pride in something that isn't mine to begin with? That would be like bragging about my new Hummer H3—right after I pick it up from Budget Rent-a-Car for the weekend. When we rightly understand that God is the owner of *all* and everything we have is on loan, our hearts will be free from pride in what we have.

In Danger of Dust

First John 2:17 lets us in on the "end" of all the world's goods: "And this world is fading away, along with everything that people crave" (NLT). When we make things and/or accolades the driving forces of our life, we'll be set to retire—eternally speaking—with squat. Not only do the trinkets and trophies collect dust, break, and become passe in this life, but we'll also have nothing to show for ourselves on the other side of death. Only those who love the Father above *all* in this life will be rewarded accordingly in the next.

Job's friend, Zophar, had some pretty sobering words for those of us who are infected with affluenza, plagued by insatiable cravings, and laid waste by pride:

They will vomit the wealth they swallowed. God won't let them keep it down. . . . They will give back

81

everything they worked for. Their wealth will bring them no joy. For they oppressed the poor and left them destitute. They foreclosed on their homes. They were always greedy and never satisfied. Nothing remains of all the things they dreamed about. Nothing is left after they finish gorging themselves. Therefore, their prosperity will not endure. In the midst of plenty, they will run into trouble and be overcome by misery. (Job 20:15, 18–22 NLT)

Is anybody else deeply convicted and conflicted over the similarities between Zophar's description and the state of our own households? How many of us are working tirelessly for things we can't keep? Why are we the most affluent society in history yet plagued by a troubling lack of joy? How many of us ignore the poor daily and instead wall ourselves into our relative castles, nestled in sanitized suburban neighborhoods? Are we greedy and never satisfied? Have you *seen* the foreclosure rate lately? If these things are true of us, then Zophar's stern predictions are sure to follow suit: nothing will remain of everything we've dreamed about; and in the midst of our plenty, we'll be miserable. I'd call that the antithesis of success.

So what *will* last? What *will* bring lasting joy? What *is* God's measure of true success?

For the answer, we go back to Job. God lauded Job because he was blameless, had integrity, feared God, and stayed away from evil. To echo John, Job's "success" was loving the things of the Father, rather than trying to replace Him with the things of the world.

The Christian "Business Model"

Even those of us who are familiar with God's Word are not immune to pride. Satan himself knew God, yet because his pride went unchecked . . . well, you know the story.[5]

Is it possible to know God—even *love* God—and yet confuse service to Him with our own ambition? Absolutely. Jesus blasted the Pharisees for giving God lip service while their hearts were filled with evil (Matt. 15:8–9). The apostle Paul also made it clear that some "do not have pure motives as they preach about Christ. They preach with selfish ambition, not sincerely" (Phil. 1:17 NLT). I'd add that some also serve on committees, lead small groups, become elders, go to seminary, travel to other continents, start ministries, record albums, become pastors, write books, and vie for TBN spots because of the same "selfish ambition" of which Paul writes.

It's no wonder, really. Pursuing "Christian" notoriety is the only way I can think of to have the best of both worlds. In the Christian "business model," we get a nod of approval from society for pursuing a path that helps change the world by "doing something good," and we can also (theoretically, at least) gain our "reward in heaven" for serving God on Earth. Success on both fronts. Or is it?

A lot of us are caught up in this religious version of the American dream, even in the church. For example, a friend of mine wanted to be a career youth pastor. But that aspiration didn't jive with his "higher ups." In fact, he was looked down on because of his lack of ambition! To be a success in the local church, apparently, you need to go to school to get your bachelors, M.Div., and possibly doctorate. Then you work your way up the ranks of a church, from youth pastor to assistant pastor, and eventually to lead pastor. Once you're on top, your job is to grow your church to a successful number. One hundred will never turn heads, so you're encouraged to "think big" and implement a "growth strategy." You're going to need at least four-digit Sunday attendance to be taken seriously at pastor's conferences. Then, once you have a few thousand in attendance and blog, Facebook, and twitter platforms, you can go on to write books. Once you have a book or two on your resume, you can speak on invitation outside your flock. If you work hard enough, you can eventually retire and enjoy all the luxuries you've accumulated through your hard work and revel in your five-star reputation.

Are the similarities between the world's and the church's "business models" as startling to you as they are to me?

Students, retirees, stay-at-home moms, single parents, middle-management employees—each of us could likely rattle off the "business model" we feel is expected of us in order to reach "spiritual success." It likely includes a mix of visible service, sacrifice, giving, teaching, going, and leading. Each of these are worthy pursuits! But as Jesus warned, we have to be careful not to practice the good things God has commanded us to do in front of an audience (Matt. 6:1). In other words, we can't let our devotion be dictated by who's watching. Living for an audience of One is at the heart of embracing obscurity.

The committed Christian's unhealthy ambitions may take different forms than you'd expect from general society, but unless our pride is intentionally and ruthlessly cut out of our lives, it can be just as dangerous—maybe even more so. That's why God gave us an entirely different business model to emulate. In the Sermon on the Mount, Jesus boldly charged us to replace the world's view of success with His when He said:

God blesses those who are poor and realize their need for him, for the Kingdom of Heaven is theirs.

God blesses those who mourn, for they will be comforted.

God blesses those who are humble, for they will inherit the whole earth.

God blesses those who hunger and thirst for justice, for they will be satisfied.

God blesses those who are merciful, for they will be shown mercy.

God blesses those whose hearts are pure, for they will see God.

God blesses those who work for peace, for they will be called the children of God.

God blesses those who are persecuted for doing right, for the Kingdom of Heaven is theirs.

God blesses you when people mock you and persecute you and lie about you and say all sorts of evil things against you because you are my followers. Be happy about it! Be very glad! For a great reward awaits you in heaven. (Matt. 5:3–12 NLT)

To get to the place where we can truly embrace our obscurity, we'll have to sacrifice our dreams of worldly success and instead take on this humble disposition. Which is, as we learned in chapter 3, the disposition of Christ.

Wrestling with Success

I'm a stinker for practicality. I suppose all of us are. I'm sure at some point you too have wished God had included a personalized book of the Bible leaving you detailed instructions about which job to take, whom to marry, what to "be," where to go, and how to do "it." And of course, I'm sure you have come to the same conclusion to which I—and thousands before me—have come: that crafty God did it on purpose. His ambiguity is, like all other things, perfectly planned with divine intent. The struggle to define what integrity, goodness, and fearing God demand in any given situation is part of the great tension and triumph of the Christian life.

If you've ever watched a wrestling match, you've seen that the very nature of the sport is grappling. The competitors hold, twist, pin, and muscle each other around until one of them gives. They are forced to embrace each other in order to wrestle. Wrestling without conflict is . . . well, it's chess. (No offense to you masters out there.) The same is true of our quest to define personal success in God-terms. Without detailed, personalized instructions, the best thing we can do is wrestle with our consciences, with God's Word, and with the Holy Spirit in these matters. The prerequisite to embracing obscurity, humility, and simplicity of lifestyle is a willingness to step on the mat.

There's no one-size-fits-all model for godly success. (Job had a fortune of wealth, Paul had next to nothing. Esther was well-known, the boy with the sack lunch remains nameless.) But we are given some guardrails to help keep us from running off the road. As I've searched the Scriptures for these guidelines, recurring themes jump out at me. They come into sharp contrast against what we've already discussed as the world's cravings. I've compiled them on the next page for contemplation.

The contenders have stepped into the ring. The match is on.

What does it look like for you and me to embrace the things of the Father? In our fast-paced world, how will we

Things of the World	Things of the Father
Make as much money as possible.	Give as much money away as possible, and spend even yourself on others.
Live comfortably.	Life is not about comfort, but about doing hard things now so that we can reap rewards in the life to come.
Make a name for yourself.	Make His name great.
Do whatever makes you happiest.	Do whatever makes God happiest.
Teach your children to behave.	Teach your children to love and obey God. ("Behaving" is often, but not always, a blessed by-product.)
Look like a model in a magazine.	Treat your body as the temple of the Holy Spirit and cultivate an inner beauty.
Offer "acts of service" when you feel like it (on your own terms).	Be a servant, even when it is uncomfortable or inconvenient.
Stay married, as long as you love your spouse.	Serve your spouse (the way Christ modeled servanthood), and choose to love him or her for life.
Come across as powerful, influential and/or interesting.	Give preference to others, in words and actions.
Use (worldly) wisdom to accrue wealth.	Value true wisdom (which is the fear of God) over all the treasures on Earth.
Stay up-to-date with the fashions.	Be content to have clothes.
Try to be good, but cut yourself some slack.	Strive to be "perfect," just as our Father in heaven is perfect.

"lead a tranquil and quiet life in all godliness and dignity" (1 Tim. 2:2)? In a society built around possessions, how will we keep from being proud of what we own? Where are we trusting in unreliable mammon? How can we instead use our money, influence, and passions to do good, be rich in good works, and be generous to the needy (1 Tim. 6:17–19)? To answer those questions, this must be our prayer:

> Make Your ways known to me, LORD; teach me Your paths. Guide me in Your truth and teach me, for You are the God of my salvation; I wait for You all day long. . . . [You lead] the humble in what is right, and [teach] them [Your] way. (Ps. 25:4–5, 9)

Free to Live

I met a man at a coffee shop this morning who was especially anxious to read the morning paper. Apparently he had entered a "Five-Word Essay" contest and wanted to see if he had won. As he tested his entries on me, one thing was clear: he was proud of his witty submissions and would be incredibly disappointed if his name didn't appear in the paper today! But, to his credit, as each entry was only five words long, he explained that he hadn't spent an exorbitant amount of time on the venture. So at the end of the conversation, he mused with a grin, "Aw, I'll be happy with an honorable mention."

One of the beauties of focusing our priority energies on kingdom work is that we don't have much to lose if our earthly pursuits don't turn out the way we hope. When we care more about serving and loving God and others than we do about achieving our goal of the week, we won't be ruffled if we go home with the "honorable mention" ribbon at work, school, or play.

You may have heard it said, "If you don't have anything to prove, you won't have anything to lose." Take it from an ex-striver: this concept, lived out, is rather revolutionary. Embracing God's formula for success frees us to really live—to try, fail, get up, and try again—because we know that "failing" in the world's eyes will never let God down. How could it? We were never holding Him up. Quite the opposite—He'll continue holding *us* up, whether or not we ever make headlines, change the world, or get our big "break."

> Commit everything you do to the LORD. Trust him, and he will help you. He will make your innocence radiate like the dawn, and the justice of your cause will shine like the noonday sun. (Ps. 37:5–6 NLT)

You want to be successful? If you live comfortably, share what you have. If you have a spouse, serve him or her sacrificially. If your home is filled with the clamor and clutter of children, savor the monumental challenge of raising them. If others follow you, point them to Christ. If you are given accolades, receive them humbly. Love and serve the people around you. Walk well through the inevitable sufferings of life. Live your life worthy of the gospel of Christ. This is true success. And really, what more could we possibly want?

> Now to Him who is able to do above and beyond all that we ask or think according to the power that works in you—to Him be glory in the church and in Christ Jesus to all generations, forever and ever. Amen. (Eph. 3:20–21)

Discussion Questions

1. Can you point to any life decisions you have made based on a desire to be successful by the world's standards?

2. Why would the apostle John say that loving God and loving the things the world offers are mutually exclusive (1 John 2:15–17)?

3. First John 2:15–17 details three categories of the world's offerings: 1) a craving for physical pleasure, 2) a craving for material things, and 3) pride in our achievements and possessions. With which of these three categories do you struggle most?

4. Given the course of your life, will you have anything to "take with you" into eternity?

5. Look at the chart on page 87. Which "Things of the World" are the most tempting to love? In light of that answer, which "Things of the Father" are most critical for you to embrace for your spiritual survival?

6. Embracing *true* success while still living in the world is tricky business. With which tenets of worldly success are you currently wrestling to give up?

7. Do you see any areas in your own life where you have confused or commingled service to God with your own ambition?

8. Can you think of any other ways society has trained us to view success?

9. How does embracing God's true measures of success free you to "fail" in the world's eyes?

10. After reading this chapter, how would you define success in your own life?

CHAPTER 6

Embracing Servanthood

*But Jesus called them over and said, "You know that the
rulers of the Gentiles dominate them, and the men of high
position exercise power over them. It must not be like that
among you. On the contrary, whoever wants to become
great among you must be your servant, and whoever wants
to be first among you must be your slave; just as the Son of
Man did not come to be served, but to serve, and to give
His life—a ransom for many."*

MATTHEW 20:25–28

*It is one thing to follow God's way of service if you are
regarded as a hero, but quite another thing if the road
marked out for you by God requires becoming a doormat
under other peoples' feet. God's purpose may be to teach
you to say, "I know how to be abased" (like Paul). Are you
ready to be less than a drop in the bucket? To be so totally
insignificant that no one remembers you even if they think*

of those you served? Are you willing to give and be poured out until you are all used up and exhausted—not seeking to be ministered to, but to minister?

OSWALD CHAMBERS[1]

I once heard cancer described as a "kind killer." *Kind* isn't the word that came to mind when I lost someone dear to me to the disease, but I can see their point: One benefit of hearing that you have three months to live is that you have three months to get ready to go. For many of the nearly 600,000 men and women who will die this year from cancer in the United States,[2] their diagnoses will give them a chance to put their "affairs in order." They can ask for an estranged daughter's forgiveness, decide who will inherit their Elvis Presley collection, and maybe scratch the most important line or two off the ol' bucket list. They can even plan their own funerals: "Open with bagpipe procession. . . . Sing 'Amazing Grace' before Uncle Jack talks . . . Make sure the minister doesn't mention so-and-so. . . . And I best be dressed in my signature navy suit!"

At the very least, most people faced with immanent death will write out a few last words. If you've ever watched the show *I Shouldn't Be Alive*, you've seen this on a dramatic scale. When all hope is lost, and some poor chap is marooned, starving, and certain that all hope of a rescue is gone, he'll go to great lengths to leave parting words for his family or friends. He'll scratch them into a shard of metal with a pocket knife if he has to. Words like, "Tell the kids I love them," or "I'm sorry. I've always loved you," burn in their hearts and also touch *us* somewhere deep inside—maybe because we suspect we would feel the same way if we were in their (unfortunately doomed) shoes.

When faced with death, everything we've ever wanted to say is boiled down, and we can then administer it to our loved ones in concentrated doses. There isn't much time. Only the weightiest matters matter, and every word must count. For that reason a person's final words are often the truest, deepest, most important of their lives.

If you knew you were going to die, what would you want to say to your spouse? Your parents? Your best friend? Your kids?

Would you take the opportunity to tell them?

Jesus did. He knew He was about to die, and He was determined to take advantage of the final hours He would share with his closest friends and loyal followers. What did He tell them? What would be of such import to share in the precious few moments allowed Him before His betrayal and death?

The Towel That Toppled the System

Of all the Gospel writers, none gives such a detailed description of Jesus' "last words" as John. Nearly a quarter of the chapters in his Gospel are dedicated to recounting them.

Five chapters.

One hundred fifty-five verses.

If a person's last words are the most poignant of their lives, Christ's final sermon is chock-full of significance. Each word carries weight in both the practical and the divine realms.

Can you imagine yourself in the upper room with Peter, John, James, and the others? Just before the Passover meal, they're wrapping up a recurring debate over their viability in the kingdom, wondering, *Who's the most valuable to this new regime?* (Luke 22:24). None of the Twelve perhaps minded not being the absolute *greatest*, as long as he wasn't considered the *least*. Tempers might have flared; certainly testosterone was wafting freely around the room. (Oh the sinfulness of *all* God's chosen!) If Christ ever rolled His holy eyes, I imagine it would have been at that moment. In the foreshadow of what was about to transpire in Gethsemane, watching the petty bickering and manipulative arguments, He may have thought to Himself, *Are you kidding me? Have you learned nothing during the past three years I've taught you the great paradoxes of the kingdom of God? Are you still entrenched in the world's system of success? Have you not yet understood the better way?* What He did next must have startled His followers even more than it does us:

> Jesus knew that the Father had given everything into His hands, that He had come from God, and that He was going back to God. So He got up from supper, laid aside His robe, took a towel, and tied it around Himself. Next, He poured water into a basin and began to wash His disciples' feet and to dry them with the towel tied around Him. . . . When Jesus had washed their feet and put on His robe, He reclined again and said to them, "Do you know what I have done for you? You call Me Teacher and Lord. This is well said, for I am. So if I, your Lord and Teacher, have washed your feet, you also ought to wash one another's feet. For I have given you an example that you also should do just as I have done for you. I assure you: A slave is not greater than his master, and a messenger is not greater than the one who sent him. If you know these things, you are blessed if you do them." (John 13:3–5, 12–17)

Luke adds to Christ's final discourse in his Gospel:

He said to them, "The kings of the Gentiles dominate them, and those who have authority over them
are called 'Benefactors.' But it must not be like that
among you. On the contrary, whoever is greatest
among you must become like the youngest, and whoever leads, like the one serving. For who is greater,
the one at the table or the one serving? Isn't it the one
at the table? But I am among you as the One who
serves." (Luke 22:25–27)

The long-awaited Messiah, washing the filth from a dozen
average guys' feet. It just felt . . . *wrong.* It didn't fit, to let the
Master do a slave's job. I can't say I blame Peter for initially
refusing Christ's act of service.

Does the servant-leader paradox feel any less unnatural to
us today? Those who practice it are rare enough that a reality
TV show like *Undercover Boss* grabs national attention. The
CEO doing entry-level cleanup? Shocking! Yet as believers we
are not given the option to do anything *but* serve. Jesus' words
echo in our hearts: "I have given you an example that you also
should do just as I have done for you." He washed His disciples' feet *so* they would do likewise for one another. We are
not exempt from this command any more than we are from
His other teachings. Don't murder. Don't commit adultery.
Serve one another as I have served you.

The mandate is clear: Among us it will be different from
the world's pecking orders. Those who desire greatness must
become experts at the art of serving the servants. Service and
embracing obscurity are so permanently and irrevocably inter-
twined, we have no choice but to master the former before

we'll be able to enjoy the latter. I do hope this chapter will whet your appetite for more.[3]

Sacrifice and a Soaker Hose

One of the hallmarks of true success (which we discussed in chapter 5) is servanthood, and judging by the portion of Jesus' "last words" He devoted to the subject, no discussion of true and lasting success would be complete without it. Similarly, in order to embrace obscurity, we must master the art of serving with humility, as nothing deals a death blow to our pride like selfless service.

For those of us trained in the world's success-omatic system, service—particularly *hidden* service—is especially difficult. I resonate with Richard Foster's take on this neglected virtue in his book, *Celebration of Discipline:*

> In some ways we would prefer to hear Jesus' call to deny father and mother, houses and land for the sake of the gospel than his word to wash feet. Radical self-denial gives the feel of adventure. . . . But in service we must experience the many little deaths of going beyond ourselves. Service banishes us to the mundane, the ordinary, the trivial.[4]

This is the great difficulty of service: dying to self. How much easier to hear and obey God's call to leave all for a tribe in Africa than to let the car to my left have the right of way. Would I feel more comfortable working for an overtly Christian ministry than to stack chairs in the break room of a secular workplace? Does my pride rear up when I consider how I might serve the way *Christ* served? Am I willing to give up my lofty ideas of success—even the "success" of serving God in great and visible ways—and instead content myself to serve in the mundane, to be largely invisible, and to meet the needs of those who can't return the favor?

These are questions I have been chewing on for some time. One evening, while watering the garden (go figure), the sheer sacrifice of *true* service overwhelmed me. There among the tomatoes and parsley, I realized that most of my previous attempts at service were much like the garden hose in my hand: I was in control, dictating how, when, and to whom I would serve. With my nifty sprayer, I could even stop the water altogether when I felt like it. The "flow" of Christ's love which I gave to others depended on my mood, the health of my career, and even how much sleep I got the night before. Mine was (and still often is) a self-righteous, self-gratifying service. In contrast I noticed a soaker hose in the planter across from me. It watered the ground completely indiscriminately. Dozens of holes let the water loose and had no shut-off switch. Life-giving water oozed out all over the place, like it or not! To serve like a soaker hose means to pour out Christ's love from every pore of our beings, not concerning ourselves with the timing, the effect it might have on our productivity, or the worthiness of the recipients. If God has "turned on the water" in our lives, filling us with His life-giving springs, why would we hold them back from anyone? For fear of running out? Doesn't He have an infinite supply of living water?

That unlikely lesson in the garden is still taking root. I'm sure not perfect, and my selfishness often gets in the way of opportunities to die to myself. But I am learning to *long for* the title given to so many faithful men and women who have gone before me—not those God calls "My successes," but rather "My *servants*": the likes of Abraham, Isaac, Jacob,

Samuel, David, the people of Israel, . . . the *Messiah*. When God wanted to give someone a real compliment, that's what He would call them: "My servant." Flipping through the pages of the Old and New Testaments, you hear Yahweh giving praise like, "for the sake of *My servant* David"; "Have you considered *My servant* Job? No one on the earth is like him"; "*My servant* Jacob, . . . without fail I will save you," and "Here is *My Servant* whom I have chosen, My beloved in whom My soul delights" (2 Kings 19:34; Job 1:8; Jer. 46:27; Matt. 12:18; emphases added).

Ironic, isn't it? We go striving for accolades to please ourselves and our Father, when He desires most for us simply to enjoy Him and let the rivers of His pleasures spill out to others. Serve Him by serving others. Meet others' needs out of the overflow He has given us, through our words, compassion, hospitality, wealth, courtesy, and all the menial tasks that get opportunity when people live in proximity to one another.

If there is great difficulty in service, there is also great delight! Serving others enables us to shake free from the world's tethers of promotion, authority, and getting an "edge," and liberates us instead to *rest*. I'm not talking about laziness but a soul-rest that brings peace no striving can produce. God wants us to break free from the shackles of self-serving and instead voluntarily take on the *beneficial* yoke of serving others. You'll find no "pecking order" in His kingdom; it was abolished in the example Christ gave.

We have looked several times at the attitude that Christ exemplified for us, found in Philippians 2:5–11, but it bears repeating:

Make your own attitude that of Christ Jesus, who, existing in the form of God, did not consider equality with God as something to be used for His own advantage. Instead He emptied Himself by assuming the form of a slave, taking on the likeness of men. And when He had come as a man in His external form, He humbled Himself by becoming obedient to the point of death—even to death on a cross. For this reason God highly exalted Him and gave Him the name that is above every name, so that at the name of Jesus every knee will bow—of those who are in heaven and on earth and under the earth—and every tongue should confess that Jesus Christ is Lord, to the glory of God the Father. (Phil. 2:5–10)

Now let's consider the two verses that precede that passage—the instructions which required Paul to teach so extensively about Christ's humility:

Don't be selfish; don't try to impress others. Be humble, thinking of others as better than yourselves. Don't look out only for your own interests, but take an interest in others, too. (Phil. 2:3–4 NLT)

Paul knew what revolutionary commands he was giving the Philippians! In order to digest and live out commands like "Don't be selfish," "Don't try to impress others," "Be humble," "Think of others as better than yourselves," and "Take an interest in others," we must acquire a living and active understanding of Christ's humility—hence verses 5–11. Only in understanding that the King of everything took the position of a *slave* can we fathom servanthood ourselves.

The Parable of the Trees

If understanding Christ's humility is the cornerstone of service, perhaps the next foundational layer could be put this way: Just because we *can* have high position or authority doesn't mean we should *choose* it.

A little gem of a parable, tucked away in a mess of Israel's sin during the time of the Judges, describes this principle:

> The trees set out to anoint a king over themselves. They said to the olive tree, "Reign over us." But the olive tree said to them, "Should I stop giving my oil that honors both God and man, and rule over the trees?"
>
> Then the trees said to the fig tree, "Come and reign over us." But the fig tree said to them, "Should I stop giving my sweetness and my good fruit, and rule over the trees?"
>
> Later, the trees said to the grapevine, "Come and reign over us." But the grapevine said to them, "Should I stop giving my wine that cheers both God and man, and rule over trees?" (Judg. 9:8–13)

The parable concludes when the trees, in their desperation for a king, ask the bramble to rule over them. The thornbush (representing Abimilech) accepts the office.

I love this parable more each time I read it. Take a look at the priorities of the first three kingly candidates. The olive tree, the fig tree, and the grape vine each turn down an office of power, influence, ease, recognition, and even usefulness, in favor of being true to their God-appointed purpose: *serving* God and man. Why should they rule over the trees when they could bless, honor, give, and cheer right where they were planted? The olive, fig, and vine each chose obscurity over fame because they understood the high calling and pleasures of service. Such wisdom in their response!

To varying degrees, each of us has opportunity to "rule over" our fellow trees. Should we take those chances when they come? Perhaps. But as the trees in the parable taught us, those opportunities should be passed up if they would inhibit our ability to serve God and our neighbor to our fullest potential. Better to forfeit position than God-given purpose; and we know for certain that we were made to serve. As Andrew Murray said, "Being servants of all is the highest fulfillment of our destiny, as men created in the image of God."[5]

What does this kind of sacrifice look like? To serve in humility, even forfeiting legitimate opportunities of "advancement" for the sake of serving? Certainly the picture will look different for each of us. Here are just a few examples of people who have inspired me with their willingness to embrace obscurity in order to take up their towels.[6]

> Tyler is a mid-level food service supervisor at a large Christian camp. After working in that role for nearly ten years, the higher-ups offered him the chance to manage all of food service (and all the perks that go with it). Tyler turned them down. He felt he could do more good serving customers and personally training younger staff—even though that meant flipping burgers with college-age kids.

> Heather taught in the public school system for five years before becoming pregnant with her first child. To the astonishment of her coworkers, she did not

return to work once her daughter was born. She now has five children and has chosen to continue staying at home to homeschool them. Not only has her decision to sacrifice her career for her children cost her the income and recognition she would have received as a teacher, but she has also "lost" her mother, who cannot forgive her daughter for her "reckless" decision.

Dan, a talented jazz musician, has chosen to use his talents in a nonconventional way. Instead of booking concerts for personal fame and financial success, Dan formed a ministry that takes music, instruments, and the hope of the gospel to underprivileged kids around the globe. Despite his musical giftedness, he lives on a missionary's salary for the sake of serving others.

Misty turned down a full-ride volleyball scholarship to CSUB in order to follow God's call to a small Christian college, forfeiting the exposure and training she might have had to play professionally after graduation.

Coach D turned down a reported forty-million-dollar contract with a leading NBA team in order to continue coaching and mentoring his college-age players. The fame and fortune of the NBA wasn't "ultimate success" in his playbook, much to the relief of his players.

I'm sure you could add a name or two of your own acquaintances to this list. Can I ask you something? Is it your goal someday to *add your own*?

Longing for Favor

*Learn the lesson that, if you are to do the work of a
prophet, what you need is not a scepter but a hoe.*

BERNARD OF CLAIRVAUX[7]

How much more appealing is a scepter than a hoe to a
mind trained to have "a craving for physical pleasure, a craving for everything we see, and pride in our achievements and
possessions" (1 John 2:16 NLT). Like the disciples, most of us
spend a whole lot of time contriving ways to move up the ladder, next to never considering movement in the opposite direction. Why? Because we want to be favored. Until now, we
may have wanted that favor from teachers, parents, coaches,
bosses, friends, or other influentials. Now, though, God has
given us a different system. We aren't to long after the *world's*
admiration any longer. Instead He gives us this command and
promise:

> All of you, serve each other in humility, for "God opposes
> the proud but favors the humble." (1 Pet. 5:5 NLT)

God *favors* the humble. I vote for Ultimate favor over the
world's any day of the week. How about you? Will you allow
your life to be spilled out for others—like a soaker hose of
God's love, a conduit of blessing and encouragement?

> Once a man has experienced the mercy of God in
> his life he will henceforth aspire to serve. The proud
> throne of the judge no longer lures him; he wants to
> be down below with the lowly and the needy, because
> that is where God found him.[8]

Discussion Questions

1. If you knew you had only a few weeks to live, what would you want to do before you died? What would you want to say, and to whom would you want to say it?

2. Based on Matthew 20:25–28, how would you describe Jesus' proverbial corporate ladder?

3. Read John 13:3–5, 12–17 again. According to verse 3, what truths motivated Jesus to serve His disciples? What truths should motivate us to serve? (See verses 14–17.)

4. Try to imagine yourself in the room with Jesus the night of the last supper. How do you think you would have responded when the Man you had been following—the Man you expected to rule Israel—got down on His knees to wash *your* feet?

5. Can you think of any other contemporary examples of someone serving those he or she is leading?

6. How does the world's success system affect our views of service?

7. Up to this point, how would you describe your attitude toward service? After reading this chapter, how has that view changed?

8. How is sacrificial service tied to embracing our relative obscurity in this life? Why is it so important to master the art of serving, especially in mundane and ordinary areas?

9. What are some of the great joys, delights, and rewards of serving? In other words, *what's in it for us?*

10. We learned from the parable of the trees (Judg. 9:8–13) that just because we *can* have high position or authority doesn't mean we should *choose* it. Can you imagine a scenario when you might have reason to turn down a position of authority in order to better serve others?

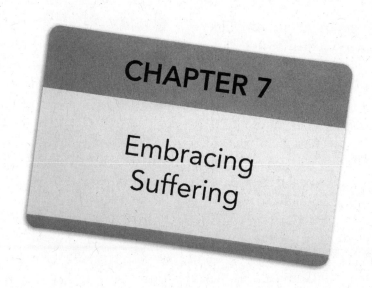

CHAPTER 7

Embracing Suffering

*Now I rejoice in my sufferings for you, and I am
completing in my flesh what is lacking in Christ's
afflictions for His body, that is, the church.*

COLOSSIANS 1:24

Share in suffering as a good soldier of Jesus Christ.

2 TIMOTHY 2:3

*Measure thy life by loss and not by gain; not by
the wine drunk but by the wine poured forth,
for love's strength standeth in love's sacrifice,
and he that suffereth most hath most to give.*

UGO BASSI[1]

Derrick[2] decided to go to seminary after college. He
loved God and wanted to serve Him in full-time ministry as

a pastor. As luck would have it, in between classes and late-night studies, he found the girl of his dreams and asked her to marry him. Respected by his parents and peers for pursuing a "spiritual" life, and now enjoying life with his bright-eyed bride, Derrick felt certain a successful career in ministry was just around the corner.

Graduation came and went, and the job hunt began. Derrick sent resume after resume, but as weeks turned into months, no job came. Churches turned him down; nonprofits too. Eventually, to support his young family, he went to work at the last place he would have expected—a local hospital— doing that last thing he would have expected: cleaning bed-pans. Not exactly what he had in mind when he committed to serve God with his life. This turn of events dealt a heavy blow to Derrick's resolve, but the menial (and—come on, now—gross!) day-to-day realities of his job changed him in ways no pastorate ever could. His ambition was ambushed, his pride pummeled, and he gained a greater appreciation for true service—the kind of hidden service we came to appreciate in chapter 6.

A Bit about Suffering

As with service, writing about suffering gives me no small amount of anxiety. It's one of those *holy grounds* of the Christian life: the subject of time-worn volumes about sainted martyrs. How many men and women in our lifetime, and of those who have gone before, could delve further into the heart of God on this matter than can I? But there's a cause-and-effect relationship between suffering and embracing obscurity that we can't afford to ignore.

In *A Path through Suffering*, Elisabeth Elliot muses, "The

word *suffering* is much too grand to apply to most troubles, but if we don't learn to refer the little things to God how shall we learn to refer the big ones?"[3] Perhaps that's why her definition of suffering seems so fitting:

> Having what you don't want, or wanting what you don't have.[4]

This is the perfect definition of suffering for our discussion about embracing obscurity because it's in the little "sufferings" of demotions, hard breaks, layoffs, out-of-state moves, and menial jobs that we learn to defer to God our dreams of being well-known, respected, and admired. It's in these trenches that we realize God is big and we are small, where we exchange our will—our dreams, desires, and plans—for the opportunity to make much of Him and less of ourselves. As you think more deeply about the role suffering plays in helping you embrace obscurity, obvious losses may come quickly to mind (e.g., the death of a loved one, a chronic illness, etc.). But I hope you'll also bear in mind: (1) the things in your life that you wish weren't there, (2) those things you want to have but don't, and (3) anything you want to be but aren't.

With those definitions in mind, let's consider two reasons for suffering: the change it brings in us and the way suffering enables us to give more to others.

Suffering Changes Us

Many of us can point to our own "bedpan" experiences. For some those down and dirty trials have been relatively short seasons; for others, suffering seems to be a way of life. Whether a relative inconvenience or a life-altering event, whether a consequence of our own sin or a divine life-lesson, we have the opportunity to allow suffering to change us. The spectrum of lessons we can learn through trials is endless really; I've tried to whittle the list down to five by focusing on ways suffering can specifically help us learn to embrace obscurity:

- **Suffering helps us learn that God's way of living is best.** As the psalmist said, "My suffering was good for me, for it taught me to pay attention to your decrees" (Ps. 119:71 NLT). Sometimes the only way for God to get our undivided attention is to put us through the proverbial wringer. Somehow suffering wakes us up to the reality that God's "decrees" are the way to go.

- **Suffering is essential to distinguish our motives.** In the quagmire of our fallen hearts, we can have a hard time differentiating between pure motives and pride, selfless service and our own ambition. As God refines us "in the furnace of suffering" (Isa. 48:10 NLT), our true motivations are revealed. Through the fire of affliction, the dross floats to the surface, and we're forced to own up to the junk we see there and deal with it.

- **Suffering helps keep us from pride.** I emphasize *helps* keep us because I don't believe we'll be able to eradicate pride completely this side of eternity. However, just like selfless service, suffering forces our pride into submission. In contrast, those who live painless lives— lives that aren't "afflicted like most people"—wear pride like a Tiffany necklace (Ps. 73:4–6).

- **Suffering often changes our ambitions.** Before his conversion, Saul cared primarily about his reputation and perfecting his religiosity. The transformed Paul left reputation behind and instead boasted in weakness, longing to suffer and share in Christ's death (Phil. 3:10). The mode of this metamorphosis? Suffering. Paul's apostleship boot camp included a direct rebuke from Jesus, blindness, beatings, shipwrecks, and "a messenger of Satan to torment [him] and keep [him] from becoming proud" (2 Cor. 12:7). Through Paul's sufferings his ambitions changed dramatically. Perhaps he sacrificed a dream of a spot in the Sanhedrin in order to make tents and preach the gospel. Others have attested that their "valley of the shadow" reminded them of the importance of family, their dependence on God, and the vanity of overworking.

- **Suffering can reveal our idols, which enables us to find God.** Naaman was a successful warrior, wealthy army captain, and the object of even the king's admiration. If he hadn't been afflicted with leprosy, Naaman likely would have finished out his days a rich, lauded hero but a lost soul. Instead, through his suffering (a severe mercy!), Naaman was led on a journey toward humility, which ultimately led him to the true God. While you and I may not worship Rimmon as Naaman had, suffering has a way of stripping away our own false gods—idols like ambition, a perfect romance, material things, and the other "things of the world" we discussed in chapter 5.

How has God allowed you to suffer? Have you lost a home? Received a startling diagnosis? Been plagued by self-doubt or troubled relationships? Longed for a dream that evades you? Suffering is inevitable. You know it; I know it. We also know that how we respond says much about us. Will we be teachable through the dark moments and difficult seasons? Will we allow God's Spirit to humble and transform us through our pain and disappointments? Will we allow our suffering to multiply what we have to offer others?

Suffering Enables Us to Give

Todd and Danika unexpectedly lost their ten-month-old daughter to a sudden illness. A few months later, as I talked with them about their loss, Danika shared how blown away they had been by the hundreds of people who supported them through that dark season with prayers, meals, books, and words of encouragement. I knew they were grateful. Then Danika mentioned a couple who had also lost their young son, and her countenance changed. She relaxed, spoke more softly—less rehearsed. As she told this other couple's story, and shared how much she hung on every word they shared about their "new normal," the reason for the connection was obvious. While Todd and Danika's story had garnered the sympathy and advice of many well-trained ministry leaders and even Christian counselors, what touched them deepest were the words of an ordinary couple who had *been there.*

Can you relate? In your moment—or season, or life-time—of hurt, were those who spoke most poignantly to your soul (perhaps without even a word) the men, women, or children who have walked in your shoes?

Have you ever noticed that there's a kind of secret society you enter once you've suffered? The particulars of your story don't matter as much as the simple fact that you and someone else have felt the same deep pain. Though initiation stinks, there are benefits to membership. Camaraderie is one. You also become more aware of other sufferers around you and feel less self-conscious about offering sympathy. You get to hear their own heart-wrenching stories and learn along with them. You get to rejoice with those who overcome. And in your own darkest moments, as Todd and Danika found, you get to draw from the deep wells of authentic wisdom that come from walking through the fire.

The first and greatest commandment is to love God with all our hearts, souls, and minds (Matt. 22:37–38). We've already seen how suffering changes you and me, enabling us to love God more fully. Yet suffering also plays a part in our obedience to the second greatest commandment: to love our neighbors as ourselves (Matt. 22:39). Through suffering we are enabled to love, give, support, stand by, encourage, and empathize with our neighbors in ways we were never able to before.

"He that suffereth most hath most to give."

We keep coming back to this truth: In order to embrace obscurity, we have to model Jesus Christ. He is our example in everything! Humility. The greatest serving the least. And now we see that He is also our example in suffering. Christ suffered much and, in turn, had much to give.

> But we do see Jesus—made lower than the angels for a short time so that by God's grace He might taste death for everyone—crowned with glory and honor *because of the suffering* of death. (Heb. 2:9, emphasis added)

Because Christ gave up divine privileges and embraced obscurity for the love of us—because He *suffered*—He not only secured glory and honor from His Father and every nation on Earth, but He was also able to give us two gifts we could never attain on our own: reconciliation with God and eternal life with Him. In view of those *ludicrathetic* truths, it seems a small sacrifice to taste of suffering in this life, doesn't it? Wouldn't we *want* to be able to imitate our Savior—not only in miniature versions of His sacrifice but also by having something to offer others for our pains?

> Through suffering, our bodies continue to share in the death of Jesus *so that* the life of Jesus may also be seen in our bodies. (2 Cor. 4:10 NLT, emphasis added)

More often than we'd care to admit, the best way to love our neighbors as ourselves is through suffering on their behalves. Isn't that the model Christ gave us? He loved us radically enough to suffer the most excruciating pain possible—separation from His Father—to rescue us. To benefit us. Christ suffered intensely, died and was raised to life, yet (even in His glory) defers benefits to us. Wouldn't you or I be the first to stand up and say, "Yeah, His suffering was *definitely* worth it"? Then shouldn't we also be the first ones to lay down our lives for others? Let someone else benefit from *our* suffering? Those who are forgiven much love much (Luke 7:47), and those who are the recipients of the benefits of suffering should be the first in line to suffer for others. Our love for and devotion to Christ, coupled with our desire to follow His example, should compel us to suffer on others' behalves with enthusiasm—with *gusto*.

Granted, we will never go through the depths of suffering that Christ did. Most of us may never even suffer any real, physical pain for someone else. So how do we "suffer as a good soldier of Christ" (2 Tim. 2:3) and participate in His sufferings on behalf of the church (Col. 1:24)? And how do our less dramatic sufferings equip us to embrace obscurity? What kind of "little sufferings" can we learn to refer to God?

I think of the guy who works for a company he really can't stand. Yet he goes, day after day, and spends eight hours between cubicle walls making phone calls and filling in data sheets. He has what he doesn't want: a so-called dead-end job with no promotion in sight. He stands at a crossroads. On one hand, he could go out and look for another job that better "confirms his worth." Or he could embrace obscurity and accept that his worth doesn't depend on the cool factor of his occupation. He could allow this daily suffering to transform him and enable him to have more to give—Christ's love, plus a wealth of compassion and patience—to his coworkers, bosses, or others who find themselves in a similar situation.

Or how about the student who feels isolated because his mysterious, gospel-driven lifestyle doesn't exactly draw a crowd of friends. Instead of partying on the weekends, this kid would rather stay sober and make it to church on Sunday morning. The suffering of a solitary life could cause him to question whether he's taking this "Jesus stuff" too far. He could wallow in self-pity because he wants something he doesn't have (namely, more friends). Or he could embrace the lessons that loneliness teach us about our own obscurity and instead cling to Christ and reach out to others for His sake.

I think also of the girl who wants nothing more than to be married yet doesn't see an end to her singleness. She wants to be something she's not—a wife and a mother—and the longing is acute. She wrestles with questions like, "Is there something wrong with me?" "Why is *everyone* married except me?" and "Am I not good enough?" She could let her suffering consume her, or she could allow her singleness to force her into the arms of Christ, finding her true significance in her Savior rather than in a husband. If she will choose the latter, her suffering will provide her with much to give! Single men and women are free to be "concerned about the things of the Lord" rather than "the things of the world," and can be "devoted to the Lord without distraction" (1 Cor. 7:32–35). In her singleness she is in an ideal spot to love and serve others through embracing her obscurity.

How about you? Think again about some of those tough times you've walked through or are walking through now. How might God be using the things in your life that you wish weren't there? Those things you want to have but don't, or what you want to be but aren't, to make you more than what you were in order to give more than what you once had?

The Joseph Principle

There's a startling trend in Christian thinking about suffering. Though subtle, this misconception is no less dangerous than many other of Satan's lies. I call it the "Joseph Principle," and it goes like this:

> If I am suffering in obscurity today, God must be preparing me for something greater, better, or more prominent later in life.

You can probably guess why I call it the Joseph Principle. I can only assume this faulty way of thinking gets its roots in a misunderstanding of Joseph's unlikely story, found in Genesis 37; 39–50. In a nutshell, Joseph is betrayed by his brothers, sold into slavery, falsely accused of attempted rape, and then endured years of prison for a crime he didn't commit.

Yet—and this is the part that excites our ambition—God used all of Joseph's suffering to prepare him for greatness (and I mean *greatness*). In a startling turn of events, Joseph becomes the second most powerful man in Egypt, ultimately saving the family that first betrayed him. In the end he gets it all: fame, power, justice, and even the girl.

Though Joseph's story is one of my favorites, there are others like it. Abraham waited twenty-five years but in the end had the child he'd been waiting for. Moses had to spend forty years as a shepherd, but he eventually went back to Egypt and was God's instrument to deliver the Israelites. Hannah put up with years of taunting and disillusionment before God gave her Samuel. David endured fourteen years of wondering, waiting, and dodging Saul, but in the end he became the greatest king Israel ever knew (notwithstanding Christ).

Why do we love these stories? Lots of reasons, to be sure. There's action, adventure, hidden identities, wrongs made right, God's faithfulness and fulfilled promises—but there's also something about the underdog making it to the top that resonates within. Maybe because we hope it will be us?

If you've ever been fired, come up second (or tenth), been broken up with, or had any hope deferred, you've likely heard the well-meaning encouragement: "Don't worry—God just has something even better in store for you!" or "All things work together for good!" or maybe even, "You just keep working hard, and you'll get what you want in the end." I guess we give one another these platitudes for one of two reasons: (1) we really believe that suffering inevitably leads to bigger and better, or (2) we hate to kick someone when they're down by telling them the hard truth: sometimes suffering only leads to our greater obscurity but God's greater glory.

The Bible is wrought with examples of God's doing things for His own glory. Refining our hearts is no exception: "I have refined you in the furnace of suffering, . . . yes, for my own sake!" (Isa. 48:10–11 NLT). He goes on to say that Isaiah doesn't want his reputation tarnished by idols; He refuses to let the recognition due Him go to them. It was true in how He dealt with Israel, and it is true in how He deals with us. God more often allows us to suffer to refine our own hearts and purge us from idols than to prepare us for "greatness."[5]

This isn't an easy pill to swallow. The simple fact is that we *like* to view every setback through the lens of inevitable success: "Rejected again? That's okay. It will only sound that much better when I'm famous to have had such humble beginnings." Or "Yeah, she dumped me, but I know God has someone even *better* lined up down the road." "I'm broke now, but God is only teaching me to manage my money wisely now so He can trust me with more later." Or, to paraphrase a popular blog post I read this morning, "My time in the 'waiting room' of life is just a season of growth and development, getting me ready for my moment on the stage." We comfort ourselves with this kind of self-talk because it's far more soothing than the thought of suffering for the sole purpose of God's glory or—heaven forbid—having to embrace obscurity *indefinitely*.

Romans 8:28 is most often used to support the Joseph Principle, "We know that all things work together for the good of those who love God: those who are called according to His purpose." This is true—absolutely true. But to freely interchange the word "good" in that verse with the world's definition of success is a gross misinterpretation. Yes, God works all—even our suffering—for our good, but the end result may well look different than you had hoped. Will you still trust God if your "good" is to go on embracing obscurity—living in simplicity and devotion to Him—your entire life? What if your "good" is to understand the deepest depths of suffering so that you have more to give to others who walk through dark times? Would you mind if your "good" is only a greater understanding of the suffering Jesus went through on your behalf and mine? What if your "good" is soley to make His name great?

All of God's ways are good and true. Although His plans may not look like ours, we can trust that God is in fact "for us." Embracing obscurity allows us to relinquish our dreams for and to Him—to His timing and His ways. We prefer Him to the dream. We don't push our dream into being.

Remember my friend Derrick? You might think that after cleaning up crap for a while, God would give the guy a break and let him pastor a church. Surely he had learned his lesson and was ready to get in the game. That's what most of us would have thought anyway, based on the Joseph Principle. But instead of giving Derrick a reprieve from suffering, God took him to new depths of it. In a heartbreaking series of events, Derrick and his wife lost their young daughter.

Isn't it tempting to think, *Surely now, God, Derrick is ready for the "big time."* Now that he has gone through the shadows and come out alive, he must be ready to do "great things" for You. He at least deserves that! But God's ways are not our ways, and His crucible isn't always to prepare us for fame or even financial stability. Derrick is still living an incredibly ordinary life, if you measure success by achieving his "goals." But I don't know anyone who has more to give his coworkers in terms of compassion, love, and truth. God has caused everything to work together for Derrick's good, and not only his but countless others whom he has ministered to in the ordinary, everyday trenches. He'd still love to be a pastor someday, but the title isn't so imperative anymore. Suffering has enabled him to lay ambition aside and only want the position if God leads him there.

Anonymous Sufferings

If we are seeking glory, honor, and immortality
before God, daily and quiet persistence,
faithfulness and obedience is the road to get there.
Anonymous sufferings are actually the best kind,
Jesus tells us—otherwise, others might recognize us and
compliment us and that, alone, will be our reward.

GARY THOMAS[6]

"Anonymous sufferings are the best kind." When I read that quote, I immediately think of Mary,[7] a single mother of five living in a small town in rural Nicaragua. Abandoned by her husband after their youngest was born handicapped (the social stigma of disability is still acute in that region), Mary has defied a poverty of heart if not of home. Yes, she's poor. She has little opportunity to get ahead of her family's most basic, daily needs, yet she does the best she can to support herself and her kids, almost always with a smile. An able and energetic woman, she has used the lessons learned through her own suffering to educate many other families about the truth of children with disabilities: that they are loved equally by God and should also be valued by their families and community.

Living in a *barrio*, without a car, TV, or Internet, Mary's suffering is largely anonymous. In fact, if I hadn't written about her here, maybe no one in the world would ever hear her story. But even if she did have access to the social network, it wouldn't matter. Mary is not ambitious like that. She's not trying to capitalize on the "sob story" market by writing memoirs or starting foundations. She's not vying for a spot on Oprah. I doubt she's ever even considered wanting an article in the local paper. Quite the opposite—she seldom thinks of herself or of her story. Almost unnoticed, she has simply allowed the lessons learned through her own suffering to spill out to others. She has more to give *because of* her pain, and she gives it freely.

Anonymous sufferings really are the best kind when we consider eternity. Just as Jesus taught us to do our acts of service and devotion privately, so also "your Father who sees in secret will reward you" for the suffering you endure anonymously (Matt. 6:18). This hope is so life changing, so revolutionary, that we're going to spend a whole chapter savoring it before this book is through. In the meantime, just to tease your taste buds a little, take a minute to really think about this truth: all suffering in this life—no matter how small or how crippling—is *incomparable* with what's to come. "Our momentary light affliction is producing for us an absolutely incomparable eternal weight of glory. So we do not focus on what is seen, but on what is unseen. For what is seen is temporary, but what is unseen is eternal" (2 Cor. 4:17–18). Bottom line: There's no suffering in this life that even comes close to overshadowing the glory that will be revealed in us (Rom. 8:18). *Amen?*

Are we willing to stop kicking against the goads and instead *embrace* the inevitable suffering in our lives? Will we stop banking on the Joseph Principle, and count it joy to share in the sufferings of Christ (however minute ours are in comparison)? When we accept our suffering as an opportunity to have more to *give* rather than *get,* humility is born. And this kind of humility—the kind Christ modeled for us—you'll remember, is the beginning of embracing obscurity.

Discussion Questions

1. How would you define suffering as it relates to our struggle to embrace obscurity?

2. With which aspect of suffering do you find it most difficult to cope: having what you don't want, wanting what you don't have, or wanting to be something that you aren't?

3. How has past or present suffering changed your view of yourself? of God? How has it changed your priorities or your goals?

4. Suffering enables us to give more to others. How did Christ model this kind of suffering for us? What was He able to give us because of His suffering?

5. How does our suffering—undramatic though it may be—equip us to embrace obscurity?

6. What is the "Joseph Principle," and how is it dangerous?

7. If suffering doesn't necessarily mean that we are being prepped for a more visible role, what good might it still do us? What benefit might our suffering bring to God? to others? to ourselves?

8. Why are "anonymous sufferings" the best kind?

9. What is our ultimate hope in the midst of suffering obscurely?

CHAPTER 8

Embracing the Mystery

For since, in God's wisdom, the world did not know God through wisdom, God was pleased to save those who believe through the foolishness of the message preached. Yet to those who are called, both Jews and Greeks, Christ is God's power and God's wisdom, because God's foolishness is wiser than human wisdom, and God's weakness is stronger than human strength.

1 CORINTHIANS 1:21, 24–25

The question is not whether *we will be seen as fools—that part is certain—but* when *and* by whom *we will be seen as fools. Better to be seen as fools now in the eyes of other people—including other Christians—than to be seen as fools forever in the eyes of the Audience of One, whose judgment ultimately matters.*

RANDY ALCORN[1]

Candace[2] gave her life to God five years ago, right about the time she started a small business. She poured as much into her venture as a wife and new mother could. Although she couldn't have admitted it at the time, Candace felt that her vocation gave her a purpose and identity that stay-at-home motherhood could not. She worked whenever her husband was home so they could tag-team caring for their young daughter without sending her to day care. Candace got cheers and many a "good for you" from clients and friends. But as her business grew, a few key relationships deteriorated—one being her marriage. When her husband, Erik, changed jobs and began working more, Candace subconsciously resented him for putting his success over hers. They no longer needed the income her business provided, yet she couldn't let it go. It was a good business, she would argue, and she enjoyed it. Late-night fights and days of silence between them became more regular and exponentially intense. After a few months of trying to keep all the pieces together, she finally reached a crux: either let go of her business or lose her marriage. She knew what was expected, what would be seen as perfectly normal; she knew what most women would deem acceptable. One choice would secure nods of approval but could quite possibly destroy her marriage; the other choice would make her look like a weakling or a lunatic but might secure peace on the home front.

Three months later Candace found herself at a mountain cabin with her husband's mother, sister, and grandma. "What's going on with you and Erik?" her sister-in-law inquired. "We can tell something's different with you guys, in a good way." Candace, surprised they had noticed, told the three women about her decision to take a hiatus—indefinitely—from her business so that she could focus on serving her husband and mending their relationship. Usually sweet Grandma just about flew through the roof. "*Serve* Erik?" she literally yelled, "Women are not *made* to serve men!" The tension in the room was as thick and sticky as a Louisiana summer. Of all people those three women should have been delighted that Candace had given up her own ambitions to serve her husband so self-lessly. He was, after all, a grandson, son, and brother to the ladies in that room. But even though Candace's in-laws could see the benefit that had come from giving up her "rights" to accomplishment to serve someone else, they couldn't figure out why anyone would be willing to *do* that. Candace's decision didn't make sense from their perspective, and the mystery literally maddened them.

The path of the Christian life often leads in the opposite direction of the world around us. First Corinthians 4:10 says, "Our dedication to Christ makes us look like fools" (NLT). If learning to embrace obscurity is part of our dedication to Christ, then becoming nothing in light of God's everything might just make us look *insane* to the rest of the world.

Our Mysterious Example

People didn't "get" Jesus.

You could argue that He intentionally remained mysterious. He spoke in parables, retreated to the wilderness, and often warned those who *did* know His true identity to keep hushed about it. But there was also much about His life and ministry that just baffled onlookers. As we discussed in chapter 6, His model of Servant King was outrageous. Counterintuitive. Madness.

No one expected the life of God-in-flesh to look so humble, so *ordinary*. The Pharisees were looking for more flashiness, greater credentials, and more obvious signs of deity. They underestimated His authority all the time. They ridiculed Him for drinking wine and eating with sinners, judged Him for healing on the Sabbath, and didn't believe He could forgive sins. Even Christ's own disciples expected a little more political ambition and a little less humiliation and *death* (see Luke 18:34; 19:11). They figured an uprising was inevitable if Jesus was going to be king. If you'll recall, Peter was still looking for a fight in the garden of Gethsemane. Imagine Peter's confusion when Jesus told him to put his sword away and then *healed* the "enemy."

Whether intentionally or because of others' projections, Christ epitomized mystery—bottom line. That begs the question: if we really resemble our Savior, why would we expect the world to "get" us either? Why would a follower sold out for Him blend in with a system dead-set on promoting self? Remember Jesus' own words,

> If you were of the world, the world would love you as its own. However, because you are not of the world, but I have chosen you out of it, the world hates you. Remember the word I spoke to you: "A slave is not greater than his master." If they persecuted Me, they will also persecute you. (John 15:19–20)

If we're going to embrace obscurity, modeling our lives after our humble King, we're also going to have to embrace the mystery that comes with the title. Now don't get your hopes up. I'm not talking about a Hugh Jackman-esque, overtly suave mystique. Nope, I'm referring to a raw, sometimes offensive, and rarely popular-with-the-masses kind of mystery. To put it bluntly, Christ says the world will hate us. Which begs another question: *If our lifestyle doesn't even raise the eyebrows of the world, what does that say about our devotion to the gospel?*

Worthy of the Gospel

If we're going to claim to be citizens of heaven, the Bible says we're responsible to "live your life in a manner worthy of the gospel of Christ" (Phil. 1:27).

What is the gospel? It's the good news. It's the best news. It's the news that, once heard, should permeate every cell of our being and affect every decision we make ever after. It's the news that fills up every longing and satisfies our deepest craving. It's the news that enables us to live our lives persecuted yet full of peace, displaced yet moving with direction, unknown by the world, but known intimately by One. The gospel is the news that makes it feasible to look like a fool today because of what awaits us for all our tomorrows. *What is the gospel?*

> For God did not appoint us to wrath, but to obtain salvation through our Lord Jesus Christ, who died for us, so that whether we are awake or asleep, we will live together with Him. (1 Thess. 5:9–10)

That's the gospel. To "walk worthy" of it means that my life should make sense in light of it. Not in light of the *world* but in light of the gospel. *Does it?* If my life were weighed against the magnificent grace and power I claim to believe, would the scale balance, or am I disproportionately self-absorbed? Do the time, energy, and passion with which I pursue my own interests match the intensity of my faith, obedience, and love for God and others? Is my life *mysterious?* Or do I live, love, and lust like the rest of the world?

When I think about living worthy of the gospel, a few examples immediately come to mind. These individuals know what it means to embrace obscurity by living mysteriously and, as a result, have baffled the world.

Glen Coffee

For most of Glen Coffee's life, football was everything. Like hundreds of thousands of young men, he dreamed of going pro. He was talented, and things seemed to be going his way. After an outstanding junior-year season as a running back for the University of Alabama, Glen decided to skip his senior year and enter the 2009 NFL draft. You'd think that the thrill of finally making it would have been the ultimate. But his big break was bittersweet.

Two years before he got drafted, Glen Coffee had given his life to Christ. His life did a 180. Football wasn't everything anymore. He didn't play for himself; he played for God. "When I was on the field, I honestly felt like if a player was trying to tackle me, he was trying to stop me from my ministry, because I knew the more media attention I got, the more I could deflect towards Him. So it was a great season. But even in having that season, I still knew in my heart that football wasn't it." Those feelings haunted him as he headed into the draft. During his first season for the 49ers, he tried to drown his nagging conscience with the "perks of the job." But the following season at training camp, he reached a crossroads.

> I was doing what the world expected me to do. What my mom expected me to do. What my grandma expected me to do. All I knew was football . . . so to say that I was walkin' away was scary. . . . So I tried to rationalize it . . . but my heart wasn't in it. And it was

hard. It was real hard. Cause when you don't listen to God's will and you do what the world expects you to do, you never reach what you're trying to reach. You're always strugglin'. You're in the water and you're tryin' to stay afloat. . . . When you fight God and you're of the kingdom, you're going to lose that battle eventually. And it's gonna wear down on your spirit; it's gonna wear down on you physically, mentally—all that. And it got to the point, man, that I just couldn't take it.[3]

One day before practice, Glen reached a crux. He knew he had to let the dream go and follow God—wherever He might lead. He cut the tape from his cleats (which he describes as "cutting off metal shackles") and retired after only one season with the 49ers. You can imagine the media's response! Some thought he was trying to cover up a failed drug test. Others figured he was just out of his mind or couldn't hack it. The possibility that someone would give up a lifelong dream because he felt God was asking him to pursue something more ordinary—it just seemed like madness. The big question on everyone's minds: why would someone walk away from the possibility of making millions in the NFL?

"People just keep asking me that, and . . . their No. 1 reason—their only reason—is money," Coffee said. "It saddens me, man. If your only focus is money, you're going to be sorely disappointed. A lot of people, they chase money. And when they get the money, they think, 'OK, what now? There's got to be more than what I'm feeling now.'"[4]

Glen's not exactly sure where God's going to lead him from here, but he's certain that this time around he's all about God's plan for his life. "Now I'm not fighting for a game; I'm fighting for souls." The thrill of success, and the pleasures that come with it, pale in comparison with living a life worthy of the gospel of Christ.[5]

Rose Mapendo

A Tutsi Congolese, Rose was a victim of intense mistreatment during the genocide in the Democratic Republic of Congo at the end of the twentieth century. After her husband was tortured and then executed, Rose was taken with nine of her ten children to a death camp where she spent almost a year and a half suffering in unimaginable conditions. Abuse. Starvation. Thirty-two women and children in a single prison cell—*with no toilet.* Rose wrestled with God. Why did He make her Tutsi? Why did He make her a woman? Why did He allow her to become pregnant right before this nightmare? She was gripped by hatred for the four men who guarded their cell. (Who would possibly blame her for despising them?) But during her time in the death camp, Rose came to peace with God's sovereignty and chose to forgive the four men who guarded and mistreated her and the others.

The time came for Rose to deliver. On the filthy concrete floor of her prison cell, in the dark, having to cut the umbilical cords with a piece of wood, Rose gave birth to twins. And as if forgiveness wasn't enough—this is *unimaginable* to the world—*she named her babies after two of the prison guards.* She wanted them to know that she was not their enemy. *Gospel insanity!*[6]

Ed Owens

Ed Owens' life creed was "work hard and play hard." His goal in life was to get rich quick and then retire on a beach somewhere. At age twenty-two, he was well on his way to achieving that dream. Touted "the youngest, most successful stockbroker" in his firm's history, he was on his fourth or fifth Porsche by the time he was twenty-seven. He wore a fur coat, illegal turtle-skin boots, and sported a gold Rolex; and though people might have guessed that he dealt in drugs rather than stocks and bonds, no one could mistake that he had made it—*big*. But Ed was a taker. He took from people in relationships, he took money, he took time, and he hoarded up his talents for himself.

Then Ed met Jesus. "Big time" lost its luster. Over the course of several years, God challenged Ed to be a giver, a generous giver. Ed's asset-management business continued to grow, but Ed and his wife began to live on less. Instead of accumulating a bunch of money for himself and for his family, he decided to put a cap on his income, give away much of his savings, downsize his luxury home, sell his hot cars, and focus on helping others physically and spiritually. Most would say Ed has given enough. Some might even say he has given too much—that his generosity is compromising his self-sufficiency. But Ed is convinced that, because of the gospel, it's a safer bet to store his treasures in heaven rather than throw money at temporal illusions.[7]

Now *that's* mysterious. There's no way Glen, Rose, Ed, or countless others would be willing to sacrifice today if they weren't driven by hope in something *other* than this life. They couldn't embrace obscurity if they weren't confident that living a life worthy of the gospel of Christ would deliver. They wouldn't embrace obscurity if their decisions always had to make sense to those around them. God's will for their lives took them down a path that didn't make sense to those around them. Embracing obscurity meant embracing mystery for the glory of God.

So how about us? Are we living mysteriously? Are our lives marked by service, sacrifice, love for others, abandonment of self, dependency on God, or genuine passion to see the lost saved? Or are we more preoccupied with the things of the world? A cool car or job? A retirement account? A higher education or some humanitarian work? Maybe even some noble things done but for the wrong reasons? Do any decisions in our lives seem mysterious to those around us? Without mystery we have to wonder whether we have embraced the ways of the Father or imitated the world.

I've often been broken by the incongruity in my life and have found new passion to do business with sin and take up my cross to follow Jesus. I want my life to testify to the weight of the gospel. I want to prefer God above *everything* else, including recognition, and live my life in such a way that it wouldn't make sense if there were no resurrection.

How about you?

By God's grace we have the *privilege* of comparing our lives to the gospel; of making sure we are walking worthy. This isn't about earning our salvation by extreme measures or trying to finagle special favors from God. We can't let our attempts to walk worthy of the gospel be driven by fear, drudgery, or guilt. Living a life worthy of the gospel—a mysterious life, indeed—should be a natural and joyful response to the crazy love God offers us. As Jesus taught, those who understand just how much they have been forgiven can't help but live lives sold out for their Redeemer (see Luke 7:41–47).

Because of the great love with which He loves us, we can ,
fully follow our Savior's example of embracing the mystery
gospel-driven lives embody.

The Great Exchange

I realize that if you've chosen to read this book, you're
probably familiar with the gospel already. So why spend this
much time talking about the gospel and what it means to live
lives worthy of it? Because a rightly reverential view of the
gospel is the only way to train our *hearts* to embrace obscurity.
Embracing obscurity isn't just another "Christian virtue" you
can pin on your Sunday best after completing X number of
hours in the church nursery or contributing a bag of grocer-
ies to a food drive. Nope, this is bigger than that. To live a
life that embraces an obscurity of heart, we're going to be
asked to make a great exchange. A permanent exchange. An
uncomfortable and unnatural exchange. And when we make
that exchange, we're going to look like *idiots*.

First, the obvious: to exchange something means that
you give one thing up and in its place receive something else.
The same is true of this exchange. Embracing the mystery
of obscurity means giving up one set of norms and adopting another set. As you read through the following lists, take
time to consider each of the prospects. You may find yourself
initially nodding in approval, but let the implications of this
exchange sink in. Try to envision how loco your life might
appear to onlookers if you choose to dive in headlong.

Embracing the Mystery May
Mean Giving Up . . .

Financial self-sufficiency. It's pretty simple: if you follow the world's pattern of success, you will likely earn more money. You may even be able to sit back and say to yourself "You have many goods stored up for many years. Take it easy; eat, drink, and enjoy yourself" (Luke 12:19). Sure, you may hear God's "I told you so" later on (see Luke 12:20), but you could garner a whole lot of good-for-you's in the meantime. Setting yourself up for life isn't mysterious; in fact, it's both acceptable and commendable to the world. As a result, self-sufficiency is, quite frankly, rarely a by-product of living worthy of the gospel.

Sway. People who push themselves to the front of the line may not win many friends, but—let's face it—they still get to stand at the front of the line. Whether the majority likes it or not, position equals power. There *is* a certain satisfaction in knowing that our will trumps others'.

Recognition. It feels good to be recognized, applauded, and respected. Have you ever felt the thrill of seeing visible results for your hard work? A title or trophy? A promotion? A building completed or a standing ovation? If so, then you know how addicting praise and recognition can be. It doesn't take much to become a junkie, but who wants to go through withdrawals?

A Dream. Jesus had a habit of calling people away from dreams when He invited them to become His disciples. He asked many of His followers to leave successful vocations, the dream of living comfortably, or even relationships. Not all His disciples are called to leave *everything*, but there is a good chance He will ask you to give up one or more things you've been dreaming about or would rather stay attached to.

Leisure Time. If you're used to having this commodity to yourself, to be spent on entertainment at will, giving up *your time* might be a deal-breaker. You may have been working for years at breakneck speeds for the future hope of retirement, long weekends, and lengthy getaways. When it comes right down to it, would you be willing to give up the hope (or reality) of substantial leisure time?

Comfort. Who doesn't like to be comfortable? We work hard to insulate ourselves against both emotional and physical pain for good reason—it doesn't feel good! Yet we're likely to have trouble "taking up our cross" to follow Jesus if we're set on avoiding the pain of the crossbeams against our backs.

Important Tasks. I recently had a conversation with a guy who was all in a sweat because something had gone wrong at work and he was the only guy who could fix it. While he ranted about having to go back to the office on his day off, I could tell that he rather enjoyed being essential. You have to admit, there is a certain rush in having "important" things to do. Remember the quote on Lillian's fridge from chapter 2? "While I get that the weight of all those hats can wear you down, at least be happy you've got something important to do."

Being Known. This is the crux, isn't it? It's like each of us has one lottery ticket. There's a chance we could be a world-changer, and we don't want to quit until we've played the game. If we can make our mark on something—*anything*—before we die, then you'd better believe we're going to take that chance. We don't want to be unknown. We want the world's approval on our lives. We want to be remembered.

There's a lot at stake, isn't there? But let's not forget the other side of the coin. We may have to give up self-sufficiency, comfort, or being known, but by embracing the mystery of a gospel-driven life, we gain even more in the long run.

By Embracing the Mystery We Gain . . .

God-Dependency. In a culture where dependency is seen as a weakness, this may not sound like a "gain" at all. But let's consider what we know of God. First, He has at His disposal all the riches—material, relational, and spiritual—of the universe. Second, He loves to give good gifts to His children. Third, He knows exactly what we need and is committed to providing it—no more and no less. How much better to be dependent on, and expectant of, God than to rely on our finite ability to take care of ourselves.

Money is a central theme in embracing gospel-driven mystery. It makes sense if you think about it. Money—and all that comes with it—is the most worshipped false god on the planet. How we view, spend, give and save God's resources, then, should look radically different from the world. To put it bluntly, how we handle God's money is intricately tied to whether we are walking worthy of the gospel. We have the ability, through money, to appear incredibly mysterious to others. If you want the world to raise eyebrows, start giving away your wealth. You want jaws to drop? Stop trying to make so much money to begin with. Now that's going to get you labeled a lunatic![8]

Spiritual Power. While earthly position does equal earthly power, those who live lives worthy of the gospel have a supernatural advantage. Through the death of Jesus Christ, we have power over sin and death (see Rom. 6:5–11), and we have authority over spiritual forces through His name (see Acts 3:6; 4:10). No, those realities might not get you a personal bodyguard or box seats at the ball game, but in both spiritual and eternal matters I'd say you have the upper hand!

God's Approval. "God opposes the proud but favors the humble" (James 4:6; 1 Pet. 5:5 NLT). As difficult as is the prospect of living without earthly praise, the thought of living without divine approval is terrifying. God's nod is far more substantial and satisfying than any title or award the world can give, and God *approves of* our obedience. No, we don't earn our salvation by living mysteriously—Christ earns the salvation we receive by faith—but when we love Christ, we obey Him (John 15:15, 23), and when we obey Him, He rewards us. Here's just one example: When we give up the hope of human recognition in humility, out of obedience to Christ, He blesses us with great peace as a reward.

An Assurance. I'll take a sure bet over a dream (which may or may not come to pass) any day. Fact 1: We know this life is not all there is. Fact 2: Those who choose to live mysteriously in this life have the *assurance* of eternal reward. Jesus said, "So the last *will* be first, and the first last" (Matt. 20:16, emphasis added). Yes, we give up our personal variation of the American dream today, but we gain a *sure* bet in exchange—one that will never crash with the stock market or go up in smoke.

Purposeful Time. While we may be forced to give up the hope of more leisure time, when we embrace obscurity we might find that we have all the time we need to focus on what's truly important. More golfing? Maybe not. But if we spend less time at the office vying for a promotion, we just might have more time to enjoy the life God has already given us. King Solomon wrote that both overworking and over-pleasuring are both "futile and a pursuit of the wind" (Eccl. 2:10–11, 22–23). Boundaries on our work and on our play can be good.

Suffering. This may not sound like a beneficial exchange either: to give up comfort and gain suffering. (That's the kind of deal you'd expect to get after watching a twenty-minute infomercial.) In terms of mystery, this exchange takes the cake. Why would anyone *choose* suffering over comfort? Because of one simple truth: "If we are to share [Christ's] glory, we must also share his suffering" (Rom. 8:17 NLT; see also 2 Cor. 1:7 and 4:10). Power over death and our eternal inheritance are *contingent* on sharing in Christ's sufferings on Earth, part of which includes being hated and misunderstood by the world.

Kingdom Tasks. We may not feel a great urgency in the day-to-day tasks of kingdom work (e.g., loving one's spouse, training children, serving coworkers, preparing to teach a Bible lesson, developing relationships with the poor and marginalized, etc.). Honestly, you probably won't feel a smidgen of self-importance at all. But the simplicity of service, love, and sacrifice bring about a peace that all the hustle and bustle of "important tasks" cannot—a deep-seated soul rest that comes from being in the sweet spot of God's design for your life. Getting to partner with God in kingdom work kind of blows our self-important tasks out of the water, don't you think?

Being Known. When we live mysteriously by embracing obscurity, we may become unknown to our former world. There's a good chance we'll be snubbed by our circle of acquaintances, connections, coworkers, and possibly even friends or family. But in exchange we become well known by God and well loved by His people. And the greatest marvel of all? We gain God's *approval*. Whatever sacrifices we make in this life will feel microscopic when we hear Him say, "Well done, my good and faithful servant," and "Come, you who are blessed by my Father, inherit the Kingdom prepared for you from the creation of the world" (Matt. 25:21, 34 NLT).

Another Caveat

So there's the exchange. But in the nature of full disclosure, there's one more sacrifice I should probably mention. If you decide to embrace the mystery of living a life worthy of the gospel of Christ, you aren't the only one who may suffer.

People you love may suffer too.

Would you be willing to embrace obscurity if it meant disappointing, inconveniencing, or upsetting others? What if it meant they had to give up some of *their* comforts, dreams, or expectations? Could you follow Christ's model of humility, service, and disregard for reputation then?

Oswald Chambers put it this way:

If we obey God it is going to cost other people more than it costs us, and that is where the sting comes in. If we are in love with our Lord, obedience does not cost us anything, it is a delight, but it costs those who do not love Him a good deal. If we obey God it will mean that other people's plans are upset, and they will gibe us with it—"You call this Christianity?" We can prevent the suffering; but if we are going to obey God, we must not prevent it, we must let the cost be paid.[9]

That's a little different, isn't it? What if embracing obscurity meant that your family members lost a well-known or well-loved circle of acquaintances? Had to move to a smaller house? Drove uglier cars? Wore older clothes? Took fewer or less expensive vacations? Accepting this part of the exchange is especially difficult for men or women who are the bread-winners for their families. If that's you, you might be wondering, *Will embracing obscurity jeopardize my family's security? Will my children resent me for not giving them more—or not being more? How would my spouse take it if we had to change our lifestyle?*

Those questions don't have easy answers. Yet at the end of the day, we have to trust that if God asks us to embrace obscurity—of heart and/or of position—we can also trust that "he will look after those who have been pressed into the consequences of our obedience."[10] We can't know what lessons God intends to teach others; only those He's teaching us. The good news is that we can be confident He "causes everything to work together for the good of those who love God and are called according to his purpose for them" (Rom. 8:28 NLT). Not "might cause" or "will cause—*if* . . ." He *does cause*. Now, how He does that is up to Him, and we may never be privy to His rationale. But—dare I say?—we were never promised obedience would be easy.

"My Burden Is Light"

Remember Candace? Ironically, while she was fighting to hold on to a business that was keeping her from enjoying the greater gifts God had given her, she spent a whole lot of time stressed out. After taxing client interactions or arguments with her husband, she would cry out to God for peace.

Peace.

We all want it, don't we?

We've been *praying* for God to bring our hearts peace. We've been begging Him to open the floodgates of heaven and give us a teaser of the rest to come. We've been yearn-ing for the "light" burden He promised, wondering whether we've misinterpreted Matthew 11:29–30 because our yokes certainly don't *feel* easy or light. Could we be the root of our own stress? Might our ambitions be to blame—at least some of the time? What if our pride—including our fear of being unknown—was keeping us from the rest Jesus promised? Would the exchange we just looked at be worth it then? Would the promise of peace trump the temptations of pride and the lure of being known?

When Jesus taught about God's kingdom, He challenged His listeners to give up chasing after. . . . Well, I suppose I should just let Him speak for Himself:

> Then He said to His disciples: "Therefore I tell you, don't worry about your life. . . . For life is more than food and the body more than clothing. . . . Can any of you add a cubit to his height by worrying? If then you're not able to do even a little thing, *why worry about the rest*? . . . For the Gentile world eagerly seeks all these things, and your Father knows that you need them. But seek His kingdom, and these things will be provided for you. Don't be afraid, little flock, because your Father delights to give you the kingdom." (Luke 12:22–23, 25–26, 30–32, emphasis added)

"Why worry about the rest?" Oh, like our reputations? Finding a mate? Choosing a school? Our financial security or our careers? This is the advantage of embracing obscurity! We can finally start living like we believe Jesus' words: God will give us everything we need. We don't have to go after it on our own. We can endeavor to walk worthy of the gospel of Christ in our relatively unknown positions. Then, "The name of our

Lord Jesus will be honored because of the way [we] live, and [we] will be honored along with him" (2 Thess. 1:12 NLT). In the end our dedication to Christ will prove anything but foolish—even if it does look ridiculous.

Discussion Questions

1. In what specific ways was Jesus Christ's life and actions mysterious to the world around Him?

2. If we are to imitate our Savior, in what ways should our lives also seem a little crazy to the world?

3. According to John 15:19–20, why does the world hate us?

4. Take an honest look at your life. Does it look strange to those who don't know Christ? Or do you blend in with the world?

5. What role does the gospel play in propelling us to embrace the mystery of living obscurely?

6. Philippians 1:27 exhorts us to "live your life in a manner worthy of the gospel of Christ." Based on what you've learned about embracing obscurity, how would you describe a life that is lived worthy of the gospel?

7. Describe the "exchange" that will likely take place for those who embrace a mysterious way of life. What would a person likely give up? What would he or she gain?

8. Embracing the mystery may mean giving up some things that we're rather fond of. Which of those categories would be most difficult for you to release?

9. Embracing the mystery also means gaining a whole lot in return! Which of those categories excites you most?

10. What role does our quest for worldly success play in our lack of peace? According to Luke 12:22–32, what is the antidote to our stress?

CHAPTER 9

Embracing the Spotlight

A person who is put in charge as a manager must be faithful. . . . For [God] will bring our darkest secrets to light and will reveal our private motives. Then God will give to each one whatever praise is due.

1 CORINTHIANS 4:2, 5 (NLT)

Every cult of personality that emphasizes the distinguished qualities, virtues, and talents of another person, even though these be of an altogether spiritual nature, is worldly and has no place in the Christian community; indeed, it poisons the Christian community.

DIETRICH BONHOEFFER[1]

Remember that small-town boy from Nazareth we got to know in chapter 3? You know—that ordinary guy who spent His days working, eating, sleeping, hanging out with

His family, and studying Scripture? Well, once John baptized Him in the Jordan River, and after a forty-day spiritual boot camp in the wilderness, Jesus' life took a drastically different turn. He began preaching more, asked a group of successful fishermen to leave everything and follow Him, and gave some wedding guests something to celebrate. Hearsay began spreading through town. Jesus started to get a bit of a reputation around Galilee.

Then, one Saturday in Capernaum, while Jesus was teaching in the local synagogue, someone started screaming out from the otherwise placid group, "What do You have to do with us, Jesus—Nazarene? Have You come to destroy us? I know who you are—the Holy One sent of God!" (Mark 1:24). Can you see the congregation's eyes widen? I imagine some turned around to see who was making the commotion. Others might have looked at Jesus to see what He was going to do. One or two may have pretended not to hear and fiddled with their tzitzis. What *would* He do?

Jesus looked straight at the man and commanded the evil spirit in him to shut up and get out! . . . And it *did*.

Whoa. No one was expecting that.

A low murmur rumbled through the audience. *Jesus just told that demon who was boss! Did you see that? This guy speaks with authority!* People were intrigued and excited about this "new teaching," so different from the ho-hum messages they were used to. The buzz heightened as they left the synagogue that day, and you might be able to guess what happened next.

News about Him then spread throughout the entire vicinity of Galilee. (Mark 1:28)

In a seeming instant, Jesus was thrust into the spotlight. And as the rest of the Gospels detail, He *embraced* it—for all the right reasons and in all the right ways.

When people do remarkable things—even kingdom things—a certain measure of fame may be inevitable. Jesus certainly didn't go chasing after it. It came to Him, and He embraced it as God's will for His life. He subsequently used His Christian-famous status to bring God's kingdom to the lost, the desperate, and the marginalized.

We've spent eight chapters trying to wrap our minds around this concept of embracing obscurity of heart and of position. But what happens if we wake up one day to the glare of a spotlight in our eyes? What if—like Moses, Joseph, Ruth, and David—God gives *us* a position of influence or authority . . . maybe for a week, maybe for a lifetime? If that happens, we too will be faced with a crossroads: *Will we use the spotlight for God's glory or our own? Will we allow the spotlight to illuminate the way, or will we be blinded by it?*

The spotlight itself isn't inherently good or evil, but being the center of attention sure carries with it a whole lot of temptation. Remember, we're all *relatively* unknown in the scope of humanity and especially in light of history, but there is a chance your name might be recognized in this life. Whether you've been a cheer captain or a movie star, a sheriff or a teacher of the year, you likely know what I'm talking about. Unless we're mentally and spiritually prepared for the challenges that come from even a moderate circle of influence, we may find ourselves out to pasture before the first go-round. If we're not careful, we might find out firsthand how easy it is to fall prey to the Saul Syndrome.

The Saul Syndrome

First Samuel 9 tells the story of another small-town guy, a handsome but timid Benjamite named Saul. Saul's dad was known as a mighty man of valor, but evidently all Saul had going for him was his *height.* We're told he was a full head taller than everyone else (1 Sam. 10:23). In an Oliver Twist-esque series of events, God chooses this unassuming Jew, from the least of all the tribes, to be king of Israel.

At first Saul was the picture of timidity (if not humility). I mean, the guy was found hiding in some equipment the day he was announced as king, for crying out loud! The promotion, so to speak, didn't affect him much at first, and he went back to life as usual—tending flocks and farming—the next day. But it didn't take long for the spotlight to illuminate some spiritual flaws, and instead of dealing with his failures head-on, Saul made excuses and hid behind his title. Eventually fame got the best of Saul, and he became a military tyrant and spiritual failure. His greed led him to disobey God's complete command. His pride led him to set up a monument to his own greatness. The spotlight got the upper hand. Life as *somebody* became more appealing to Saul than holiness, and he "turned away from following [God]" (1 Sam. 15:11).

The Bible says that God *regretted* making Saul king. Saul let the spotlight blind him to his own shortcomings, and he failed *miserably* as a result. So God took away Saul's throne, his position of authority, and gave it to "a man after His own heart" (1 Sam. 13:14 NLT).

None of us are immune to the temptations of the spotlight.

I've watched pastors, athletes, CEOs, and musicians, insurance salesmen, models, and interns develop the Saul Syndrome. Been blinded myself a time or two. It's startlingly easy to let the admiration of others desensitize us to the ugliness of our hearts *and not even realize it.* And if we don't want to fail—either discreetly or by being literally removed from our position as was Saul—we've got to learn how to embrace obscurity even while all eyes are on us.

You might not think you need this chapter. Maybe you're already a pretty humble leader. But let me tell you, folks, we could *all* use the reminder. Why? Because we are never in more danger of glossing over our pride than during our time in the spotlight. The danger of self-deception is acute. *I have good motivations,* we reason, *to expand my platform. I'm only looking for more influence so I can point more people to Christ.*

Are you *sure* you want to bank on that?

Jeremiah 17:9 warns that "the heart is more deceitful than anything else and desperately incurable—who can understand it?" Ain't that the truth! Most of us have less noble (albeit largely unintentional) motivations to lead and be known. The (sort of) good news is found in the next verse: "I, Yahweh, examine the mind, I test the heart to give to each according to his way, according to what his actions deserve." First Corinthians 4:5 also reminds us that God is a master at exposing our private, less noble motives. Good news for those of us committed to letting God expose our junk so that we can deal with it. Bad news if we ignore the ugly truth until judgment day!

While having our splinters dug out by a Holy God might not feel pleasant at the moment, I think we'd all agree that it's far better to let God deal with our subconscious pride than let it fester undetected. So whether or not you think you need the following, let's at least admit that when we've got a spotlight glaring in our eyes, sometimes it's hard to see straight, and we could all use some help avoiding the Saul Syndrome.

Jesus said that to those who are entrusted with more (which includes "more" influence and authority), even more will be expected (Luke 12:48). These are high stakes! If we want to hear God say, "Well done, good and faithful servant," after our tenure in the spotlight, we can't just wing it. We have to be intentional about: (1) remembering our roots, (2) remembering our purpose, and (3) remembering our limits.

Remember Your Roots

You'll recall from 1 Corinthians 1:26–29 (NLT) that it was no great compliment when God called you.[2] That didn't change when you got a promotion or produced a song. Yes, you can be excited about those things, but your significance to God never was and never will be based on your accomplishments. Just because you've now done something "important" doesn't mean you weren't just as foolish, powerless, despised, or worthless (in the world's eyes) when God chose you to be His. Do you remember why? Verse 29 reminds us that the whole reason God chooses the nobodies of this world—like you and like me—for His kingdom work is so that "no one can ever boast in the presence of God" (NLT). "If you want to boast, boast only about the LORD" (v. 31 NLT). God wanted to make sure that the hood we came from (literally or otherwise) would keep us from getting big heads about our present and future successes.

Let's say it together now: *I am not that important* (see Gal. 6:3). (There, that wasn't so bad, was it?)

We started with nothing. We're going to leave Earth with nothing. And everything we have between now and then—our stuff, our relationships, and our influence—is a gift from God. "For who makes you so superior? What do you have that you didn't receive? If, in fact, you did receive it, why do you boast as if you hadn't received it?" (1 Cor. 4:7). In other words, you and I are no different from anyone else. *Really.*

Are you catching this? Do you *believe* it?

We don't *deserve* special privileges, luxury living, or a higher level of respect from others because of our talents or bank accounts. We can't excuse snobbiness, hoarding, or passive-aggressive pride because we won the popular vote or appeared in *Adventure* magazine. Some privileges and accolades may come in our lives, but if we start feeling *entitled* to them, we're already flirting with the Saul Syndrome. All our successes and all the earthly rewards that come with them are from God. It's *all* from God. We can't pretend we're ultimately responsible for our success any more than a homeless man can ultimately blame society for his homelessness.

Part of remembering our roots means recalling often that God can use anyone and *anything* to accomplish His purposes and make His glory shine. The sick and lame, the lost and bruised, the drunk, the prostitute, and the priest have all been part of His divine conspiracies. During His triumphal entry Jesus said that if the people kept silent, even the rocks would scream out the truth of His glory. And . . . does Balaam's donkey ring a bell? I'm just sayin'. Clearly, you and I are not essential. So the fact that God has chosen to infuse us with talents and consecrate us for service to Himself— despite where we've "come from"—should keep us eternally and *humbly* devoted.

Dietrich Bonhoeffer points out, "Because the Christian can no longer fancy that he is wise, he will also have no high opinion of his own schemes and plans. He will know that it is good for his own will to be broken."[3] Remembering where we came from should put us in our place every time.

Remember Your Purpose

While working at a big summer camp one year, a friend of mine became a local legend with the campers. "Ace" was like the pied piper for grade-school kids. Everywhere he went, a train of peppy preadolescents followed. Each Sunday afternoon, a half dozen kid-crammed buses would arrive, and every following Saturday those same kids would leave devoted Ace fans.

On Saturday afternoons Ace would climb onto each bus to say so long to his little groupies. And every time he boarded a bus, he would take the opportunity to plant seeds in those young lives. "How many of you want to be like me when you grow up?" he would ask loudly. No kidding—*every* hand would shoot into the air. (Don't you just love kids' lack of inhibition?) "Then be like Christ," he would tell them. "Everything good you see in me is because of Jesus. Everything else isn't worth anything." Their solemn faces would hint that they intended to do just that. If Ace loved Jesus, then they would too.

Ironically, Ace got some flack that summer from some of the leaders at camp because they thought he was being too cocky. But when asked, Ace would tell you that he chose to *embrace* the spotlight because he knew those kids were going to idolize *something,* and he saw his brief position of influence as a means to steer them in the right direction—toward God.

Ace understood his purpose during his time in the spotlight: not to make much of himself but to make much of God.

Whether you're a camp counselor or an international celebrity, your day in the spotlight has equal purpose. We'll get to that purpose in a moment, but first let's remind ourselves what our purpose is *not.* We know these truths, but how quickly we forget them in the daily hum of success-hunting all around us. It's hard to remember that it's not about us when so many voices are shouting that it *is*. I've posted a copy of this list where I will see it each day, because I need the reminder. Maybe you do too?

- My purpose is not to *praise myself.*
- My purpose is not to *make my name great.*
- My purpose is not to *get rich.*
- My purpose is not to *gain authority over others for my ego's sake.*
- My purpose is not to *leave brothers and sisters in the dust of my ambition.*
- My purpose is not to *make others feel small.*
- My purpose is not to *become self-sufficient.*
- My purpose is not to *earn a five-star rating from the masses.*

Ratings. Is there anything that *isn't* rated these days? Cars, restaurants, gadgets, businesses, singles, vacation destinations . . . I recently checked the Amazon ratings on several *toothbrushes*, just to make sure I wasn't about to buy the "lemon." Our obsession with ratings has changed how we view all sorts of things—including how we view our own success and others'. It's so easy to start comparing what we see as our star rating with the next guy or gal's, and before we know it, we've spent hours comparing "products." We think, *Oooh, she has a huge blog following. Definitely four stars on the content. . . . But he sure knows how to deliver a punch line. I give him an extra star for that. Or, I've got to get my ratings up after that failed business proposal last week. Ted is going to pass me up if I don't.* The obvious danger in these rating games is that our purpose gets muddled in the competition. Instead of working together for a common goal (God's glory), we either get all high and mighty (when we think we achieve those coveted five stars) or wallow in self-pity and doubt (when we can't seem to get past 2.5).

> Pay careful attention to your own work, for then you will get the satisfaction of a job well done, and you won't need to compare yourself to anyone else. For we are each responsible for our own conduct. (Gal. 6:4–5 NLT)

Yes, we should model ourselves after those who are walking worthy of the gospel, but we are only *responsible* for our own conduct. Since we'll be held accountable for only those resources God has given us to invest—not what He has given others—our purpose is not to get a five-star rating in our niche but to become all that God has asked us to become in His kingdom (see Luke 19:11–27). Which might be, in traditional ways, *less* than we are now.

If we could boil down the purpose of our time in the spotlight, we might narrow it down to three points: The purpose of my influential position is to make *God's name great, to advance His kingdom on Earth,* and to *serve others.*

Purpose 1—Make God's name great. Everything God does is for His own name's sake, including creating humans. Consequently our chief purpose on this planet is to glorify our Maker. We can do that in all sorts of ways, like understanding His nature, enjoying His gifts, or telling others what He has done. While in the spotlight, we have a unique platform for the latter. Like King David, the shepherd boy who found himself in the great assembly, we shouldn't be able to stop telling people about God's "constant love and truth" (Ps. 40:10). David couldn't hide the news about God's righteousness. He talked incessantly about God's "faithfulness and salvation" to anyone who would listen. This is the same David, you'll remember, who didn't blush at dancing in his skivvies along the roads of Jerusalem, dancing in worship like a madman (see 2 Sam. 6). Can you imagine our president, dancing next to naked through the streets of Washington, DC because he was so unabashedly God struck? Now I'm not saying America wants to *see* that, but I think you get the picture. Our purpose in the spotlight is to deflect others' praise heavenward, making less of ourselves to make much of our God. May we echo David in his defense, "It was before the LORD . . . and I will be even more undignified than this, and *will be humble in my own sight*" (2 Sam. 6:21–22 NKJV, emphasis added).

Purpose 2—Advance God's kingdom on Earth. At every opportunity we can use our positions of influence to lead others to the same saving grace that God offered us through Jesus Christ. We should preach it when we can and live lives that *reflect* the gospel every day. Some of us may also be in positions of enough influence to affect global change that mirrors the things God cares about most: justice, mercy, equality, freedom, and love. The greater our earthly position, the greater our potential to join in God's master plan of spreading His kingdom on the earth.

Purpose 3—Serve others. Remember the parable of the trees from Judges 9? (If not, see page 101.) The olive, fig, and vine were wise to turn down position and prestige because they were better able to serve others and God in their obscurity. But could it be that sometimes we are better able to serve others *through* positions of influence? For some that answer will be yes, and if we do find ourselves in a position of power or influence, what an opportunity to model servant leadership! Embracing the spotlight with an obscurity of heart allows us to baffle the world with a counterintuitive, God-focused, self-denying, *humble* fame. Can you imagine the possibilities if we chose to use our positions to serve *others* rather than ourselves?

Remember Your Limits

The third key to avoiding the Saul Syndrome is to know and remember your limits. Contrary to how you might feel, you do in fact have physical, intellectual, emotional, and moral breaking points. You weren't handed a cape along with your fans. You are still the same finite individual you were back in grade school. Sounds simple enough, but much harder to remember when others expect (and even demand) so much of you. (And then there's that pesky star rating bumping around in your brain—*If I say no will I lose half a star?*)

In the spotlight only the humble will survive the long-haul. To avoid burnout and maximize your ability to be a servant-leader, here are four phrases to memorize:

I don't know everything.

Apollos was a gifted and passionate speaker and an influential believer. Yet when confronted with some errors in his teaching, he was humble enough to take theology lessons from a tentmaker and his wife. We all have room to grow, and in order to learn, we have to love instruction and correction (see Prov. 12:1), no matter what sources God uses. Understanding our limitations means that we'll ask for others' feedback, weigh their opinions carefully, and give up "our way" often.

I have limited time and energy.

As Jesus' fame spread, "He often withdrew to deserted places and prayed" (Luke 5:16). Christ was surrounded by legitimate need—urgent pleas for healing, thousands of barren souls, twelve men to prep for establishing the worldwide church—and He was the only one who could do the job. So if *He* prioritized downtime, shouldn't we? Reflection, prayer, and rest aren't luxuries to be afforded *someday* but essential elements to our survival in the spotlight today. We need space and solitude to continually establish our connection with our Lifeline and allow Him to help us prioritize our tasks, great and small.

I'm not morally invincible.

Sin is enticing. Doesn't matter whether you're a high school worship leader or Billy Graham. And while God hates sin just as much whether you're a temp worker or a state senator, people in the spotlight are undoubtedly held to a higher standard. James 3:1 reiterates, "Not many of you should become teachers in the church, for we who teach will be judged more strictly" (NLT). (I'd expand "teachers in the church" to include anyone who holds an influential position over other believers.) Ecclesiastes 10:1 explains why: "Dead flies make a perfumer's oil ferment and stink; so a little folly outweighs wisdom and honor." People who should know better, *should know better.* And when we mess up, our sin steals credibility from God's message in a bigger way. It's the ugly truth. Christian leaders, athletes, politicians, pastors, and even reality-show contestants have to establish even stricter personal boundaries and play it safe in some of the "gray areas" of morality. Better to err on the side of caution than to wind up another shameful headline in the morning paper.

I'm not irreplaceable.

Remembering our limits also means adopting an attitude of replaceability. Let's go ahead and say it together one more time: *I am not that important.* I'm not trying to be pessimistic here—just realistic. God doesn't need me and He doesn't need you. He can get the job done (any job) without us.

Like Saul, God often removes those who don't guard themselves from the dangers of pride, greed, lust, etc. But your time of influence might be a short season even if you do play by all the rules. Fame is fleeting. Embrace your moment in the spotlight while you're in it, and don't question God when the time comes to step backstage. "For [His] thoughts are not your thoughts, and your ways are not [His] ways" (Isa. 55:8). Even if we never know God's reasoning, we can trust that He is acting in *His* best interest and ours when He causes the curtain to close on even our best efforts.

Humility in the Spotlight

At that time the disciples came to Jesus and said, "Who is greatest in the kingdom of heaven?" Then He called a child to Him and had him stand among them. "I assure you," He said, "unless you are converted and become like children, you will never enter the kingdom of heaven. Therefore, whoever humbles himself like this child—this one is the greatest in the kingdom of heaven. (Matt. 18:1–5)

This passage holds one last key to help us avoid the Saul Syndrome and to embrace the spotlight in the right ways and for the right reasons. I've read this passage dozens of times, completely missing the responsibility implied in Jesus' words. For some reason I always limited these verses to mean that I had to have a childlike *faith*. That to enter the kingdom of God I had to trust God with all the innocence of a bright-eyed toddler, or to love God with the abandon of a child for his father. While those things are true, that wasn't the only point of Jesus' words. He was also answering a question. A question that came up surprisingly often.

The disciples weren't asking who would *get into* heaven (though Jesus explains the requirement anyway). They wanted to know who was going to be *greatest*. The twelve were back to star ratings. They wanted to know who was going to have the best position, the most honor, and the greatest influence when Jesus came into the earthly power they thought was coming. So Jesus showed them a child, and He told them who will be greatest: the one who *humbles* himself like a child.

The thing that sticks out to me about this passage is that Jesus gave an active command. We are to humble *ourselves*. In other words, it's not something done *to* us, like: "Let God's Spirit humble you." Though we can't do it without the transforming power of the Holy Spirit, the responsibility is on *me* to take on the unassuming, submissive, unassertive nature of a child. I not only have to *choose* humility; I have to *work* at it. And no one has to work at humility like a man or woman thrust into the spotlight. Not many of us will wake up to be international sensations, but most of us will hold some level of influence during our lives. Make no mistake, Jesus is talking to *us*. (Remember—fight self-deception!)

Without humility we will fail. We'll fall prey to the Saul Syndrome and be rendered ultimately ineffective for the task God gives us. In order to remember our roots, our purpose, and our limitations, and ultimately to thrive as *servants* in authority, will take a huge measure of grace from God. Whether or not you find yourself in the spotlight today or twenty years from now, will you pray now, asking Him for the grace to embrace it well?

Great and influential Father, how well I know that everything I have is from You—even the relatively high positions You have entrusted to me in this life. Teach me Your ways so that I can make Your name great, not my own. Help me use my positions of influence for the good of others. Don't allow me to fall to temptations that would take me out of the game. If fame or fortune would undermine my integrity, then keep me from it—or take it from me—before any damage is done to me or to others. You are more important to me than any star rating. I love You. Amen.

Discussion Questions

1. What dangers does a person face when he or she is thrust into the spotlight?

2. How might people use their positions of influence for God's glory?

3. How would you describe the Saul Syndrome? Do you know anyone who has fallen prey to it? Have you?

4. According to 1 Corinthians 1:26–29, why does God use the foolish, weak, and insignificant things of this world for His purposes?

5. How does remembering our roots keep us humble as leaders?

6. How do you tend to compare yourself with others? Why are those comparisons dangerous?

7. What are three of our primary purposes while in the spotlight?

8. Name four limitations that confine each of us. Which is hardest for you to remember?

9. What role does humility play in helping us thrive while in the spotlight?

CHAPTER 10

Embracing Hope

For our momentary light affliction is producing for us an absolutely incomparable eternal weight of glory. So we do not focus on what is seen, but on what is unseen. For what is seen is temporary, but what is unseen is eternal.

2 CORINTHIANS 4:17–18

He will give eternal life to those who keep on doing good, **seeking after the glory and honor and immortality that God offers.** *But he will pour out his anger and wrath on those who live for themselves, who refuse to obey the truth and instead live lives of wickedness.*

ROMANS 2:7–8 (NLT, EMPHASIS ADDED)

*Any temporal possession can be turned into everlasting
wealth. Whatever is given to Christ is immediately
touched with immortality.*

A. W. TOZER[1]

What's the hardest thing you've ever done?

Take a minute to think about it. Skim back over your
life, from earliest childhood to today. I'm not talking about
something that someone did *to* you but something you chose
willingly to do. What was the hardest thing? An ascent? A
degree? Birthing a baby? Getting out of debt? Making amends
with someone who shredded your heart?

Now . . . what made you do it? What caused you to go
through the hard work—the blood, sweat, and tears? What
propelled you to face the late nights, grueling training, or risk
of failure?

What was in it for you?

If you get down to the root of your motivations, you'll
likely find the hope of a reward for your efforts. Maybe you
did it to enjoy a majestic view, or for prestige, money, freedom, or peace. Maybe it was as simple as knowing it would
feel good to face a fear or conquer an unknown. Does doing
something hard for some sort of reward automatically make
you a selfish person? No, it makes you human. And guess
what—*Christ was human too.*

A Greater Reward

Hebrews 12:2 says that Christ endured the humiliation
and pain of the cross precisely *because of* the joy awaiting Him.
He did it because of His confidence in the hope of future
glory and honor: being seated beside His Father's throne for

all eternity. As you read Isaiah 53:10–12 below, look for other specific rewards God promised Christ for His suffering.

> Yet when his life is made an offering for sin, he will have many descendants. He will enjoy a long life, and the LORD's good plan will prosper in his hands. When he sees all that is accomplished by his anguish, he will be satisfied. And because of his experience, my righteous servant will make it possible for many to be counted righteous, for he will bear all their sins. I will give him the honors of a victorious soldier, because he exposed himself to death. He was counted among the rebels. He bore the sins of many and interceded for rebels. (NLT)

Many descendants . . . long life . . . prosperity . . . accomplishment . . . satisfaction . . . honors . . . Savior to many . . . Christ had *much* to look forward to in completing our redemption! Would Jesus have chosen obscurity, humiliation, and death without the promise of future reward? I don't know. But it doesn't really matter, does it? The good news is that He didn't have to choose rewardless suffering, and neither do we. God has promised reward to all those who forgo pleasure in this life *for His name's sake.*

I warned you that you'd become familiar with Philippians 2:5–11 by the time you're done reading this book. Let's look at it one more time together, this time paying special attention to verses 9 through 11.

> Make your own attitude that of Christ Jesus, who, existing in the form of God, did not consider equality with God as something to be used for His own advantage. Instead He emptied Himself by assuming

the form of a slave, taking on the likeness of men. And when He had come as a man in His external form, He humbled Himself by becoming obedient to the point of death—even to death on a cross. *For this reason God also highly exalted Him and gave Him the name that is above every name, so that at the name of Jesus every knee will bow—of those who are in heaven and on earth and under the earth—and every tongue should confess that Jesus Christ is Lord, to the glory of God the Father.* (emphasis added)

Hebrews 12:2 makes it clear that Jesus *knew* what reward awaited Him before He ever chose to come to Earth. Does that cheapen His sacrifice? No way! Neither does it cheapen the sacrifices we make in this life when we make them for God's glory (which, incidentally, is also for our ultimate good). We can go ahead and look forward to our rewards. It's OK—*we're allowed!* We can even make decisions today that will affect the *level* of our rewards in heaven (Matt. 16:27; 1 Cor. 3:11–15). God doesn't see that as selfish or hedonistic; it's just *wise.* Jesus told us to store our treasures in heaven (Matt. 6:20). That's the safe bet. That's the *sure* hope.

"Forego today to enjoy *even more* tomorrow." Isn't that the inscription on so many gifts God gives us? Sex is just one example. How many people—young and old—refuse to wait for the appropriate time and place (i.e., within the marriage relationship) and so miss out on the full spectrum of pleasures God intended? If we wait to unwrap the gift in the right context, enjoyment is heightened. The same is true of glory, honor, and immortality. God intends us to have it *but not in this life.* Not in these bodies, where sin can so easily taint our enjoyment and warp our discretion. "Being known" is one of the gifts we can forego today, and tomorrow, and the rest of this life—to enjoy the full spectrum of pleasures forevermore.

> He will give eternal life to those who keep on doing good, seeking after the glory and honor and immortality that God offers. (Rom. 2:7 NLT)

God will give eternal life to each of us who trusts in Christ and who trades the hope of being somebody in *this* life for the hope of glory, honor, and immortality in the next. When we stop living for ourselves now, and instead obey the truth of God's Word, so much more awaits us on the other side of death.

So what exactly are we looking forward to in heaven? What are the eternal rewards that so completely overshadow everything we can see, touch, and experience on Earth?

- The curse won't exist (Rev. 22:3).
- We will be reunited with believers who have gone before us (1 Thess. 4:14–18).
- It is a place of abundant joy and pleasure because of God's presence (Ps. 16:11).
- There will be no grief, crying, or pain (Rev. 21:4).
- New Jerusalem, the city of the King, will be unlike any beauty we experience on Earth (Rev. 21:10–11, 18–21).
- God's glory will be enough light to replace the sun (Rev. 22:5).
- Heaven will be full of song, and we will worship God with people from every tribe and dialect (Rev. 5:9–14).
- We will find rest for our souls (Heb. 4:9–11; Rev. 14:13).

- We will have new bodies that, like Christ's, won't ever die again (Phil. 3:21).[2]

Those things are certain, *but I know there's more.* There are endless glorious realities about heaven that aren't even *mentioned* in our Bibles. How could they be? How could God convey in human language, to *fallen* beings, the glories of pure, sinless, immortal life? Couldn't happen. Besides, God loves surprises. I wouldn't doubt that He has kept secret some of the best details just to see the look of complete awe on our faces when we see it all for the first time.

Obviously what He *has* told us about our reward is absolutely enough. Just the promise of eternity in His presence (in His *presence!*) makes embracing obscurity—and every other sacrifice in this life—worth it. Amen? As David said, "When I awake, *I will be satisfied* with Your presence" (Ps. 17:15, emphasis added). To know that there's even more awaiting us isn't just the icing on some cake—it's like getting the keys to the bakery!

> So if you have been raised with the Messiah, seek what is above, where the Messiah is, seated at the right hand of God. Set your minds on what is above, not on what is on the earth. For you have died, and your life is hidden with the Messiah in God. When the Messiah, who is your life, is revealed, then you also will be revealed with Him in glory. (Col. 3:1–4)

"Set your minds on what is above." So simple, yet—man!—how a heavenward mind-set will fuel our quest to embrace obscurity. "Set your minds on what is above," because if you are Christ's, "you also will be revealed with Him in glory." Jesus endured the cross because of the joy awaiting Him. Likewise, we can gladly stop yearning for the things of this world because of the joy awaiting *us.*

Immortal Sacrifices

We all want to be somebody. We all want to make our mark on something—*anything*. Over the course of human history, how many billions of lives have been spent yearning for earthly significance and historical indelibility? One of the greatest ironies of all time is that when we give up the hope of earthly fame and fortune, and instead embrace the obscurity of a life given in service to Christ, we are immediately touched with immortality and are assured eternal glory. *Eternal* glory. Did you catch that? If you embrace obscurity, you *will* be known. You *will* have honor and respect. You *will* rule. And the more you give up those things in this life, the more you will have them in the next. Better still, we'll then have the sinless wherewithal to use those gifts righteously, ever for God's glory.

The A. W. Tozer quote that opened this chapter bears repeating: "Any temporal possession can be turned into everlasting wealth. Whatever is given to Christ is immediately touched with immortality." That includes our bank accounts and our stuff, but also our reputations, degrees, dreams, awards, accomplishments, and accolades. Even those subtitles we love so much can be given to Him. It's a simple equation: We give it to Christ; we get eternally rich. We try to hoard those things in this life, and we'll be paupers in the next.

Understood this way, obscurity in this life—either assigned or chosen—is actually a great gift. A *great* gift. Our anonymous sacrifices get touched with immortality. By serving others now, we get credited with serving Christ later. By choosing to live mysteriously in this life, we'll live like kings for eternity. Seen that way, the decision to wait for our reward seems like a no-brainer. But the only way embracing obscurity makes sense is when we keep our eyes focused on heaven. For the equation to make sense, the imminence of eternity must outshine the lure of fame today. Forever has to eclipse the day-to-day desires and pursuits of our ordinary lives.

Does it?

Can you say for yourself what was said of Moses,

> By faith Moses, when he had grown up, refused to be called the son of Pharaoh's daughter and chose to suffer with the people of God rather than to enjoy the short-lived pleasure of sin. For he considered the reproach because of the Messiah to be greater wealth than the treasures of Egypt, *since his attention was on the reward.* (Heb. 11:24–26, emphasis added)

In this journey of learning to embrace obscurity, I've become somewhat of a reward-monger. And why not? If God didn't mean for us to calculate future reward into our present decisions, He wouldn't have told us what we have to look forward to. If my highest aim is to glorify God by enjoying Him forever, then my ultimate hope is the place and state of being when I will be able to do that to my full potential—*forever.* How much easier it is to give up all the things I once held dear when I know for certain that I will get back all I give up, *divinely supersized!*

A Sure Hope

Let's go back to the question you answered a few pages ago: *What's the hardest thing you've ever done?* When you got to the finish line, was the end result all you had hoped for? When it was all said and done, did you feel a tinge of disappointment? Did you feel let down, even a little?

Too often in human experience, anticipation gives way to disappointment. We wait and wait for some great thing—like a promotion, vacation, new toy . . . even a marriage—but the realization of it actually pales to the thrill of hope we had previously. Usually the morning after the celebratory shindig, life-as-usual feels even more bland than it did before. Not this time. *This* hope, the hope of heaven, cannot disappoint. In fact, all that we have to look forward to in the life to come will blow every expectation out of the water.

You will die. Maybe today; maybe fifty years from now. How will you spend the seconds, hours, days, and years you have left? Will you waste your time loving the things of this world, worrying about your star rating, and focusing on your success? Or will you invest the remainder of your life "seeking after the glory and honor and immortality that God offers"? Will you take on the disposition of Christ, submitting to God's will, loving justice and mercy, serving selflessly and loving fully? Will you *walk worthy* of the glorious gospel—even if no one ever knows your name?

> Lord, remind me how brief my time on earth will be. Remind me that my days are numbered—how fleeting my life is. You have made my life no longer than the width of my hand. My entire lifetime is just a moment to you; at best, each of us is but a breath. We are merely moving shadows, and all our busy rushing ends in nothing. We heap up wealth, not knowing who will spend it. And so, Lord, where do I put my hope? *My only hope is in you.* (Ps. 39:4–7 NLT, emphasis added)

Discussion Questions

1. How did you answer the first question in this chapter: *What's the hardest thing you've ever done?* What were your motivations for doing it?

2. What was the hope—the *reward*—that propelled Christ to live, suffer, and die?

3. What rewards has God promised those who forgo pleasure in this life for His name's sake?

4. Sex is an example of a gift that God gives with the inscription "Forego today to enjoy *even more* tomorrow." Can you think of any others?

5. By foregoing glory, honor, and immortality in this life, what awaits us in eternity?

6. Name five characteristics of heaven that await believers. Which heavenly rewards excite you most?

7. A. W. Tozer said, "Any temporal possession can be turned into everlasting wealth. Whatever is given to Christ is immediately touched with immortality." Which of your possessions, titles, or relationships would you benefit from giving to Christ?

8. Why is obscurity—either *assigned* by God or *chosen* by yourself—actually a great gift?

9. What truths have you learned, or been reminded of, that will help you embrace your own obscurity?

Notes

Introduction

1. I've actually wrestled with that predicament myself but have come to the conclusion that nixing the words *me, myself,* and *I* would only make for pretty bland writing.

Chapter 1

1. US Census Bureau, World Population Clock, http://www.census.gov/main/www/popclockworld.html, accessed July 10, 2012.
2. Edward O. Wilson, photographs by David Littschwager, "Within One Cubic Foot: Miniature Surveys of Biodiversity," *National Geographic* (February 2010).
3. Dr. Jason Lisle, chapter 1: "The Splendor of God's Creation, Taking Back Astronomy," as printed at Answers in Genesis website, http://www.answersingenesis.org/articles/tba/splendor-of-creation, accessed December 29, 2009.
4. Thomas à Kempis, quoted in Dietrich Bonheoffer's *Life Together* (New York: HarperCollins, 1954), 94–95.
5. *Merriam-Webster's Collegiate Dictionary, Eleventh Edition,* s.v. "obscure."

Chapter 2

1. "John Piper's Upcoming Leave," John Piper, *Desiring God Christian Resource Library,* http://desiringgod.org/resource-library/taste-see-articles/john-pipers-upcoming-leave, accessed June 8, 2010.

Chapter 3

1. Elisabeth Elliot, *A Path through Suffering* (Ann Arbor, MI: Vine Books, 1990), 39.
2. *The History Channel Encyclopedia,* "Alexander the Great," http://www.history.com/encyclopedia.do?articleId=200647, accessed January 3, 2010.

3. Michael H. Hart, *The 100: A Ranking of the Most Influential Persons in History*, rev. ed. (New York: Citadel, 2000).

Chapter 4

1. Hopefully, "La Chureca" (as the Managua City Dump in Nicaragua is locally known) will one day no longer be home to its two thousand residents (and thousands more whose likelihood depends on revenue from the trash) because of the compassion of the Spanish government, which has committed to close the dump and provide programs for those displaced.
2. *Merriam-Webster's Collegiate Dictionary, Eleventh Edition*, s.v. "valuable."

Chapter 5

1. Randy Alcorn, *Money, Possessions, and Eternity*, Eternal Perspective Ministries (Carol Stream, IL: Tyndale, 2003), 419.
2. Barna Group, "Morality Continues to Decay," November 3, 2003, http://www.barna.org/barna-update/article/5-barna-update/129-morality-continues-to-decay, accessed December 1, 2011.
3. Barbara O'Neill, "Book Review: Affluenza: The All-Consuming Epidemic" (2nd Edition), *Journal of Financial Counseling & Planning*, volume 19, issue 1, 70, accessed April 18, 2011.
4. A. W. Tozer, *The Pursuit of God* (Camp Hill, PA: WingSpread Publishers, 1958), 22.
5. If you're not familiar with the connection between Satan's pride and his fall from God's favor, read Ezekiel 28:17 and Isaiah 14:12–15.

Chapter 6

1. Oswald Chambers, *My Utmost for His Highest*, "Are You Ready to Be Poured Out as an Offering?" (Grand Rapids, MI: Discovery House Publishers, 1992), February 5.
2. "Estimated New Cancer Cases and Deaths by Sex for All Sites, US, 2010," American Cancer Society, Inc., Surveillance and Health Policy Research, http://www.cancer.org/acs/groups/content/@epidemiologysurveilance/documents/document/acspc-026210.pdf, accessed May 15, 2011.
3. For a list of resources that teach further about selfless service, visit http://www.embracingobscurity.com.
4. Richard Foster, *Celebration of Discipline: The Path to Spiritual Growth* (San Francisco: HarperCollins, 1978), 126–27.
5. Andrew Murray, *Humility* (Springdale, PA: Whitaker House, 1982), 7.
6. The names of these individuals have been changed. While I cannot vouch for

the authenticity of each person's faith, each credits God as the reason for his or her sacrifice.
7. Bernard of Clairvaux, quoted in Richard Foster's *Celebration of Discipline*, 126.
8. Dietrich Bonhoeffer, *Life Together* (New York: Harper & Row, 1954), 94.

Chapter 7

1. Ugo Bassi, quoted in Elisabeth Elliot, *A Path through Suffering* (Ventura, CA: Regal Books, 1990), 66.
2. Name has been changed.
3. Elisabeth Elliot, *A Path through Suffering*, 56.
4. Ibid.
5. This is not to say that God never uses suffering to prepare a chosen servant for the spotlight. But while God specifically gave men like Joseph, Abraham, and David early promises of future leadership, He has given most of us no such assurance. Luckily for us average folk, our obscurity doesn't undermine the fact that God has a specific and deliberate plan for each of our lives!
6. Gary Thomas, *Sacred Marriage: What if God Designed Marriage to Make Us Holy More than to Make Us Happy?* (Grand Rapids, MI: Zondervan, 2000), 150.
7. Name has been changed.

Chapter 8

1. Randy Alcorn, *Money, Possessions, and Eternity* (Carol Stream, IL: Tyndale, 2003), 419.
2. The names in this story have been changed.
3. CBN.com video interview with Glen Coffee, "Why Glen Coffee Walked Away," see http://www.cbn.com/media/player/index.aspx?s=/vod/SB103v2_WS, accessed December 2, 2011.
4. Michael David Smith, "Glen Coffee: NFL Ruins a Lot of Lives," NBC Sports, May 22, 2011, see http://profootballtalk.nbcsports.com/2011/05/22/glen-coffee-nfl-ruins-a-lot-of-lives, accessed December 3, 2011.
5. Glen readily admits that following God and playing football are not mutually exclusive. God has a different curriculum for each of us. For Glen, following God's call led him away from the NFL. Others have followed God's call by staying. In either case God often calls us to operate in a different paradigm from what the world would expect. Sometimes following God just doesn't make sense to onlookers!
6. Information taken from *Mapendo New Horizons*, www.mapendonewhorizons.org, multiple pages, accessed December 1, 2011.
7. Ed Owens, "Following Jesus with Wealth," published by Generous Giving, no date given, see http://library.generousgiving.org/articles/display.asp?id=83, accessed December 2, 2011.

8. If you're ready to be challenged to view money in a God-honoring, world-defying way, you can find a list of relevant resources at http://www.embracingobscurity.com.

9. Oswald Chambers, *My Utmost for His Highest* (Westwood, NJ: Barbour and Company, 1963), 11.

10. Ibid.

Chapter 9

1. Dietrich Bonhoeffer, *Life Together* (San Francisco, CA: HarperOne), 108.

2. If that doesn't ring a bell, you might want to glance back at chapter 4.

3. Dietrich Bonhoeffer, *Life Together*, 95.

Chapter 10

1. A. W. Tozer, *Born After Midnight* (Harrisburg, PA: Christian Publications, 1959), 107.

2. This is by no means an exhaustive list. There are dozens of references about heaven in Daniel, Isaiah, and many New Testament books, not to mention the twenty-two chapters of Revelation.